Therapeutic Massage

Therapeutic Massage

A practical introduction

DENISE WHICHELLO BROWN

Eagle
Editions

A QUANTUM BOOK

Published by Eagle Editions Ltd
11 Heathfield
Royston
Hertfordshire SG8 5BW

ISBN 1-86160-371-1

QUMAITM

This book is produced by
Quantum Publishing
6 Blundell Street
London N7 9BH

Printed in Singapore by
Star Standard Industries Pte Ltd

contents

A BRIEF HISTORY

The ancient healing art of massage is undoubtedly the oldest form of physical medicine. In China there are references to massage in the oldest recorded medical text the Nei Ching written by the Yellow Emperor.

Historical records show that massage therapy was practised widely amongst the Greeks and Romans.

In ancient Rome, Julius Caesar, who suffered from neuralgia

> "Rubbing can bind a joint which is too loose and loosen a joint that is too rigid."
>
> (Hippocrates, the 'Father of Medicine,' 5 BC)

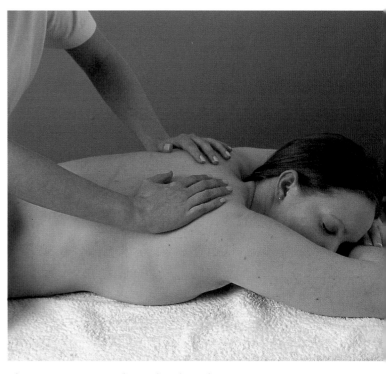

Thereapeutic massage is today much in demand

and headaches, received daily massage. Pliny, the renowned Roman naturalist was treated for his asthma. Galen, the Roman Emperor's physician, prescribed massage to prepare the gladiators for combat and to treat their injuries.

After the decline of the Roman Empire there is very little physical medicine recorded until the Middle Ages. Fortunately interest was revived by the French physician Ambrose Paré, who established the credibility of massage amongst the medical profession.

The classical technique known as 'Swedish massage,' which is described in this book, was developed by the Swedish Professor, Per Henrik Ling (1776-1839). He established a school of massage in Stockholm and in 1877, Swedish massage was introduced to the United States by Doctor Mitchell. Massage began to increase in popularity.

At the present time there is a rapidly growing demand for therapeutic massage. It is widely practised in clinics, health clubs

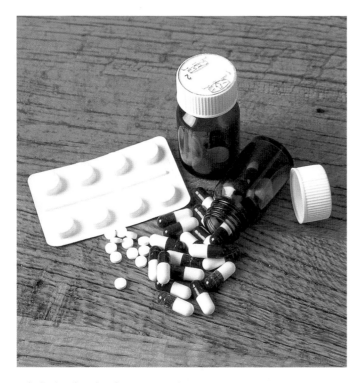

The healing benefits of massage complement orthodox medecine.

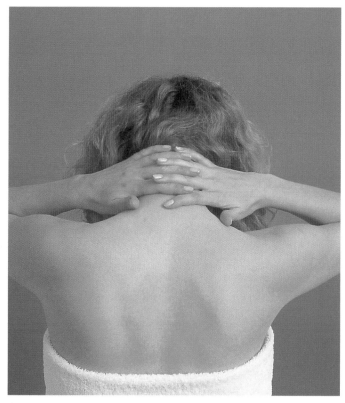

Neck massage can soothe headaches

and even in many hospitals and hospices. Thousands of therapists have trained, including lay people as well as doctors, nurses, midwives, osteopaths, chiropractors and physiotherapists who incorporate therapeutic massage into their work. The healing language of touch may complement all forms of orthodox medicine. We ALL have the power in our hands to massage and help others using the simple techniques described in this book.

THE BENEFITS OF MASSAGE

Therapeutic massage has an enormous impact on all the systems of the body.

THE NERVOUS SYSTEM

Massage can have a very powerful sedative effect on the nerves, melting away the stresses and strains of everyday life. Headaches can be relieved, patterns of insomnia broken and states of anger, impatience and irritation are soothed.

THE MUSCULAR SYSTEM

Muscular aches and pains, fatigue and stiffness can all be successfully treated with the healing art of massage. Cramp is reduced; old scar tissue broken down and good muscle tone can be induced.

THE SKELETAL SYSTEM

Disorders of the skeletal system, such as arthritis, benefit enormously from massage. Stiffness of the joints is alleviated and pain can be reduced considerably.

THE CIRCULATORY SYSTEM

Massage is excellent for improving the functioning of the heart and circulation. After a series of treatments, poor circulation improves sometimes dramatically and blood pressure falls.

THE LYMPHATIC SYSTEM

Accumulated waste substances are rapidly eliminated by the action of massage. Swellings, which may accumulate around an injury, can also be dispersed.

THE RESPIRATORY SYSTEM

Mucus and bronchial secretions can be loosened and eliminated from the lungs by performing percussive movements over the upper back and opening the chest.

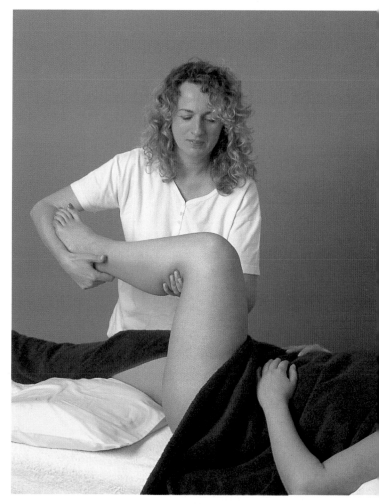

Joint pain, like arthritis, can be alleviated through massage.

Gentle abdominal massage is exellent for digestive problems.

THE DIGESTIVE SYSTEM

Massage encourages the elimination of waste matter from the colon. Constipation is relieved and digestion improved.

THE REPRODUCTIVE SYSTEM

Menstrual problems such as PMS, period pain, irregular menstruation and the menopause will all improve with regular therapeutic massage.

getting Started

Massage can be performed by anyone with very little equipment. The basic requirements are a firm massage surface, towels, cushions, a bottle of oil and of course a pair of hands. However if you can create the right atmosphere then maximum benefit can be derived from the treatment.

Make sure you have plenty of towels to hand to cover the reciever.

ENVIRONMENT
Your room should be warm and cosy, as relaxation is impossible if you feel cold. As the body temperature will drop during the massage, a good supply of spare towels and blankets is essential. Areas that are not being treated should always be covered up.

Soft and subdued lighting will create the perfect setting. Dim the lights or light a few candles around the room. Fresh flowers or essential oils add a pleasant aroma to the atmosphere and crystals such as rose quartz enhance the ambience.

It is vital to choose a time when you will not be disturbed. Take the telephone off the hook and tell your family and friends not to enter the treatment room. You may like to play some relaxing music or alternatively you may prefer silence.

PERSONAL PREPARATION
1. It is essential to wear comfortable and loose fitting clothes preferably something with short sleeves as you will get very warm and you need to be able to move around easily.

2. Take off all jewellery as rings, bracelets and watches can scratch the receiver.

3. Make sure that you trim your fingernails down as far as possible - digging the nails in is hardly therapeutic. Always wash your hands prior to the treatment and check that nails are scrupulously clean.

4. Spend a little time prior to the treatment consciously relaxing yourself. A calm state of mind is very important since if you are feeling angry or depressed it is highly likely that these feelings will be communicated to the receiver. Allow all your tension to float out of the body so that the healing energies can flow through your hands.

Carrier oils or essential oils should be used during a massage treatment.

A face ring brings added comfort for the receiver when they are lying on their front.

MASSAGE SURFACE

You will need a firm yet well-padded surface. If you are massaging on the floor, place a thick duvet or two or three blankets down onto the floor. You will require a cushion to kneel on so that your knees do not get sore. If the receiver is lying on their back place one pillow under the head and another one under the knees. If the receiver is lying on the front one pillow should be placed under the head and shoulders and another under the feet. Do not use a bed for your therapeutic massage, as these are never the correct height and therefore could make your back ache.

A professional therapist will work on a massage couch. If you find that you are doing lots of massage then it might be a good idea to invest in a portable couch. They are reasonably priced and can be erected anywhere in the house and folded away after use taking up little space. Use plenty of cushions to keep the receiver comfortable. A face ring is ideal to support the receiver's head when they are lying on their front. The massage techniques are much easier to perform on a couch and you will not tire so quickly. The massage techniques in this book are demonstrated using a massage couch.

Always ensure that you cover up any part of the receiver that is not being treated.

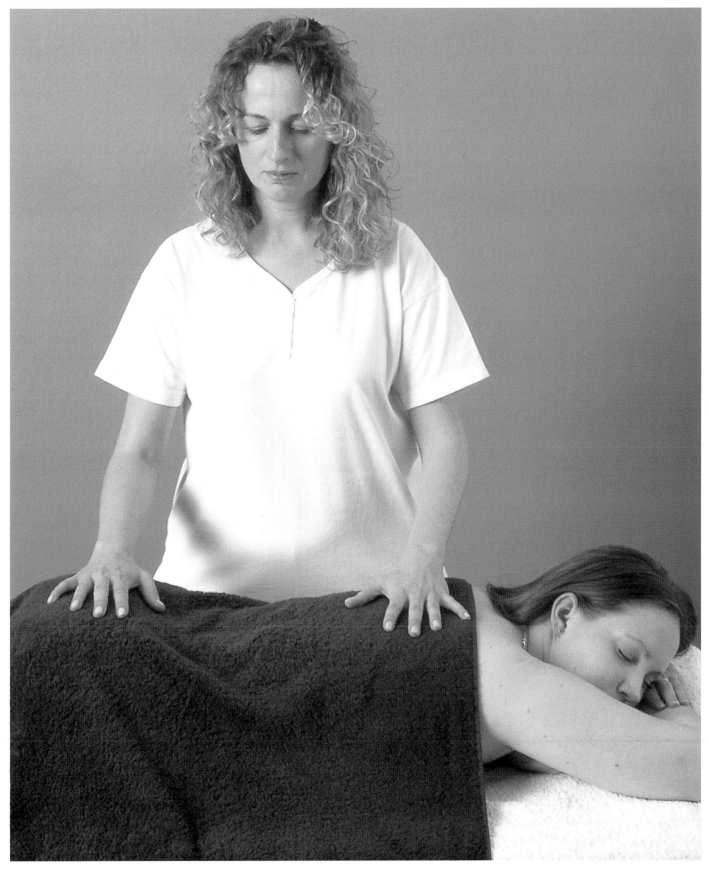

A massage couch is a useful tool as it is the correct height to allow the masseur/masseuse to work comfortably

CONTRA-INDICATIONS

WHEN NOT TO MASSAGE AND WHEN TO EXERCISE CAUTION

Although therapeutic massage is an extremely safe complementary therapy, there are times when massage is inappropriate or even dangerous. If you are at all unsure then always seek the advice of a medically qualified doctor. Please observe the following contraindications at all times:

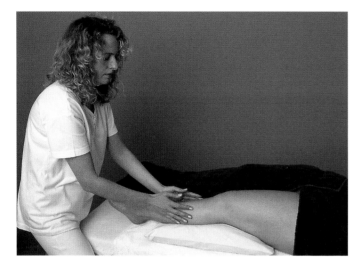

1. PHLEBITIS AND THROMBOSIS
Phlebitis is the formation of a clot in a vein that causes it to inflame. This gives rise to severe pain, redness, heat and swelling. If a thrombosis (i.e. a clot) forms in a vein, massage could dislodge the clot causing a fatal stroke or a heart attack.

2. SEVERE VARICOSE VEINS
Massage is a wonderful therapy for the prevention of varicose veins. However, if they are severe they should be avoided since you may cause a great deal of pain and further damage to the vein. Massage should be given above and below the affected area.

3. INFECTIOUS DISEASES
If the receiver has an infectious or contagious disease such as scabies, ringworm, chicken pox or shingles, then massage is not advisable. A rise in temperature is an indication that the body is fighting off toxins and massage should be avoided so that more toxins are not released into the system.

4. AREAS OF SEPSIS
Never massage over an area in the presence of pus – e.g. a boil or a carbuncle.

5. RECENT SCAR TISSUE AND WOUNDS
Massage is highly beneficial over old scar tissue since it helps to break it down and increase mobility. However, massage over a recent scar or wound can cause it to open up or become infected. Only when the site has fully healed should massage be performed.

6. INFLAMMATORY CONDITIONS
Areas of inflammation should never be massaged whether it is inflammation of a joint, muscle, skin or organ. Inflammatory conditions include bursitis (housemaid's knee), tendonitis, gastro-enteritis and nephritis (inflammation of a kidney).

7. PREGNANCY
Massage is invaluable during pregnancy since it induces deep relaxation, relieves aches and pains, improves sleep, prevents varicose veins, fluid retention and stretch marks, balances mood swings and encourages a strong bond between mother and baby. However, special care should be taken over the abdomen during the first three months if there is a history of miscarriage.

8. LUMPS
Although lumps are usually innocent, it is always wise to have them checked out by a medically qualified doctor.

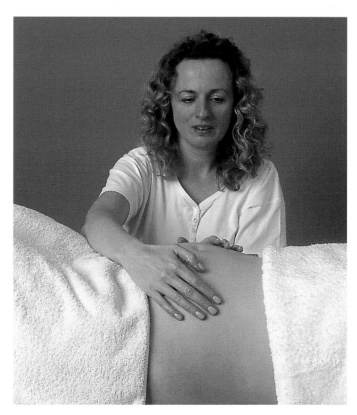

During the first three months of pregnancy take extra special care over the abdomen.

using Massage Oils

It is essential to use some form of lubricant for your massage to ensure that the hands can glide smoothly over the skin. Massage without any medium is uncomfortable and causes skin irritation, particularly on a hairy body.

Sweet almond oil is the most commonly used carrier oil.

A pure, good quality vegetable, nut or seed oil is recommended. This should be cold pressed (not removed by chemicals), unrefined and additive-free. Such carrier oils contain vitamins, minerals and fatty acids and therefore nourish the skin. Mineral oil, such as commercial baby oil, should never be used since it is not easily absorbed, lacks nutrients and tends to clog the pores. There are a vast number of base oils to choose from and it is a good idea to experiment with several to determine your personal preferences.

The most widely used carrier oil is sweet almond oil, which is easily absorbed by the skin and is not too thick or sticky. It also does not have a strong odour. It is suitable for all skin types and is beneficial for dry, sensitive, inflamed or prematurely aged skin. Apricot kernel and peach kernel oils are also excellent for all skin types and are highly nourishing, although they are more expensive. If you wish you may add thicker, richer oils to make a blend of carrier oils. These oils are usually too heavy and sticky to be used alone, as well as more expensive. However, they do improve absorption and nourish the skin. Suitable carrier oils include calendula, evening primrose and jojoba which are usually added in up to a 10% dilution. Wheatgerm oil is normally added up to 10% as it is an anti-oxidant and helps to preserve the life of a blend.

Although there are hundreds of essential oils, and a professional aromatherapist would use up to 60, only eight of the most common essential oils are described here.

The use of oils allows for a smooth and comforting massage.

CHAMOMILE, ROMAN (*ANTHEMIS NOBILIS*)

EFFECTS:
- Balancing
- Calming
- Soothing

USES:
- All nervous disorders, including anxiety, depression, insomnia and irritability.
- Female disorders, particularly PMS and menopause.
- Aches and pains whether in muscles, joints or organs, e.g. stomach-ache, backache, headache, arthritis etc.
- Sensitive and allergic skin conditions.
- Digestive problems, especially where there is inflammation – e.g. irritable bowel syndrome.
- An excellent remedy for babies and children – asthma, colic, skin problems, temper tantrums.

CONTRA-INDICATIONS:
None

GERANIUM (*PELARGONIUM GRAVEOLENS*)

EFFECTS:
- Balancing
- Healing
- Uplifting

USES:
- Wonderful for the nervous system; dispelling anxiety and depression.
- PMS and menopause – geranium balances the hormones and reduces mood swings, hot flushes and fluid retention.
- Excellent for all skin types – dry, oily, combination or inflamed.

CONTRA-INDICATIONS:
None

EUCALYPTUS (*EUCALYPTUS GLOBULUS*)

EFFECTS:
- Relieves coughs
- Expels catarrh
- Pain relieving

USES:
- All respiratory disorders. An excellent chest and throat rub and a wonderful inhalant for sinusitis and catarrh.
- Eases the pain of arthritis, rheumatism and all muscular aches and pains.
- Stimulates the brain, aiding concentration.
- Prevents infectious diseases from spreading.

CONTRA-INDICATIONS:
Do not use on babies and children under the age of 2. (Use chamomile or lavender instead)

LAVENDER (*LAVENDULA ANGUSTIFOLIA*)

EFFECTS:
- all conditions – lavender is the universal healer!

USES:
- Highly beneficial for the nervous system, combating anxiety, depression, insomnia, irritability and panic attacks.
- Reduces high blood pressure.
- Headaches, migraine, arthritis, muscular aches and pains – reduces pain and inflammation, relaxes and tones.
- All skin care. Heals burns, sunburn, acne, eczema, cuts and bruises. Highly recommended for babies and young children due to its gentle action.

CONTRA-INDICATIONS:
None

LEMON (*CITRUS LIMONOUM*)

EFFECTS:
- Alkaline
- Antiseptic
- Detoxifying
- Stimulating

USES:
- Excellent for the digestive system, especially in cases of indigestion and hyperacidity.
- Boosts the immune system and accelerates recovery from illness.
- Cuts and wounds, warts, verrucae and oily skin.
- A popular choice for varicose veins.

CONTRA-INDICATIONS:
Avoid strong sunlight immediately after application.

MANDARIN (*CITRUS AURANTIUM*)

EFFECTS:
- Refreshing
- Revitalising
- Tonic

USES:
- An uplifting oil which dispels anxiety and encourages feelings of joy and hopefulness.
- Tonic for the digestive system, stimulating the appetite and relieving indigestion.
- Excellent for pregnancy particularly to combat stretch marks.

CONTRA-INDICATIONS:
Avoid strong sunlight immediately after application.

PEPPERMINT (*MENTHA PIPERITA*)

EFFECTS:
- Cooling
- Digestive
- Pain relieving
- Stimulating

USES:
- All digestive problems especially nausea, travel sickness and inflammatory conditions such as irritable bowel syndrome.
- Headaches and migraine – cools and relieves pain.
- Cools down sunburn and relieves itching.
- Excellent for relieving arthritis, rheumatism and sports injuries.

CONTRA-INDICATIONS:
Store away from homeopathic medicines.
Do not use on babies and children under the age of 2.

ROSEMARY (*ROSEMARINUS OFFICINALIS*)

EFFECTS:
- Detoxifying
- Restorative
- Stimulant

USES:
- Clears the head, reducing mental fatigue and aiding concentration.
- A wonderful tonic and pain reliever for the muscles and joints.
- Encourages hair growth.
- Excellent for coughs, colds, sinus problems and catarrh.
- Recommended for the digestion particularly where detoxification is required – e.g. constipation, food poisoning and obesity.

CONTRA-INDICATIONS:
Do not use excessively in the first stages of pregnancy or in cases of epilepsy.

A typical example of a blend that should allow you to carry out approximately 10 treatments could be:

70mls sweet almond oil
10 mls (two teaspoons) calendula
10 mls (two teaspoons) jojoba
10 mls (two teaspoons) wheatgerm

Pure essential oils can be added to enhance your massage treatment, although they should be respected and used with great care. They are extremely concentrated and should always be blended with a carrier oil in the following dilution: three drops of essential oil to 10 mls (two teaspoons) of carrier oil or six drops of essential oil to 20 mls (four teaspoons) of carrier oil.

APPLYING THE OIL

Make sure that you always keep the oil within easy reach whilst carrying out your therapeutic massage. Once you have made contact with the receiver it is important that you do not break it, as this will destroy the continuity of the massage. Your oil may be kept in a flip top bottle or, if you are using essential oils, a small bowl is ideal. Always warm cold hands before you start. Oils should never be poured directly onto the body. Pour a small amount onto the palm of one hand and then rub your hands together to warm the oil. Then bring your hands down and begin

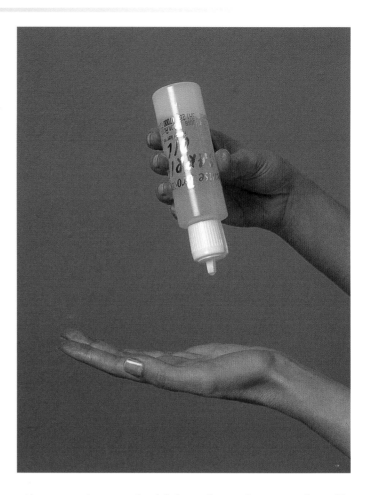

Always pour oils into your hands before applying to the receiver – this enables you to warm the oil before use.

to apply the oil using gentle effleurage movements. When you require more oil, try to keep one hand in contact with the body. It is very common to use too much lubricant when you first start. This is not only uncomfortable and sticky but it makes it impossible for you to make proper contact and perform the basic therapeutic massage movements.

Prue essential oils may be added to your carrier oil to create your own blends.

Massage Techniques

basic

The beauty of massage is that it is so simple and natural that anyone can learn how to perform it. There are four basic techniques used in a therapeutic massage. Other techniques are just a variation on these movements. Once you have mastered these you can begin to create your own strokes and develop your own personal style. Do not concern yourself too much with the 'correct' technique. The most important thing is that the massage should feel good to the receiver. Your movements should be flowing and rhythmical and you must not lose contact with the receiver as your hands flow from one movement to the next.

EFFLEURAGE

Effleurage is a stroking technique that is always performed both at the beginning and at the end of a massage. Stroking is vital as it allows the receiver to become accustomed to your hands and is used to apply oil to each part of the body. It also enables you to flow smoothly from one movement to the next.

Effleurage can be used on any part of the body and is usually performed towards the heart to assist the flow of blood. The palmar surfaces of one or both hands are used as you move slowly along the body, while moulding your hands to the contours of the body. Your hands should be completely relaxed if they are to mould to the curves of the receiver.

Effleurage should feel like one continuous movement to the receiver as you apply firm pressure on the upward stroke and glide back to your starting point with no pressure whatsoever.

Try to maintain a steady rhythm and avoid any jerky or abrupt movements that could make the receiver feel nervous and irritated. Experiment with different amounts of pressure – your movements may be soft and gentle or firm and deep depending on whether you want to work on the superficial or the deeper tissues of the body. Different rhythms can also be used. A slow rhythm will soothe and relax the receiver whereas a fast rhythm will stimulate an area.

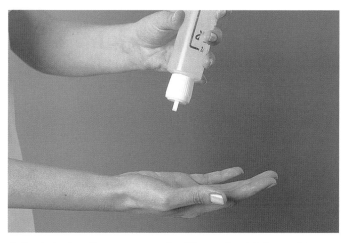

Before beginning effleurage, prepare the oil in your hands before applying

Close your eyes as you effleurage to heighten your sensitivity and intuition.

The back is an excellent area on which to practice your effleurage movements.

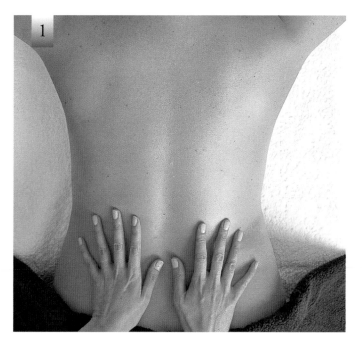

STEP 1. Position yourself to the side of the receiver and place your relaxed hands on the lower back area, one hand either side of the spine.

17

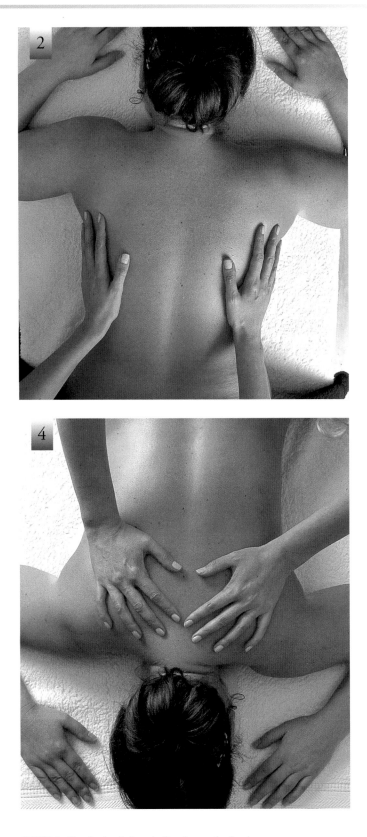

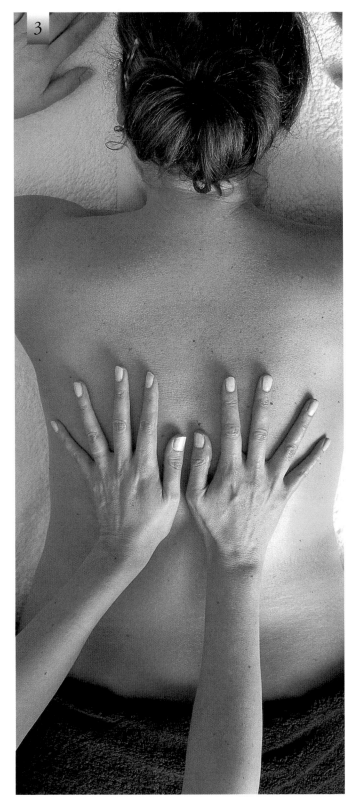

STEP 2. Stroke both hands firmly up the back

STEP 3. As your hands reach the top, spread them outwards across the shoulders.

STEP 4. Allow them to glide back without any pressure. Repeat this movement several times to accustom the receiver to the feel of your hands. Try experimenting with different pressures and rhythms and ask the receiver what he /she prefers.

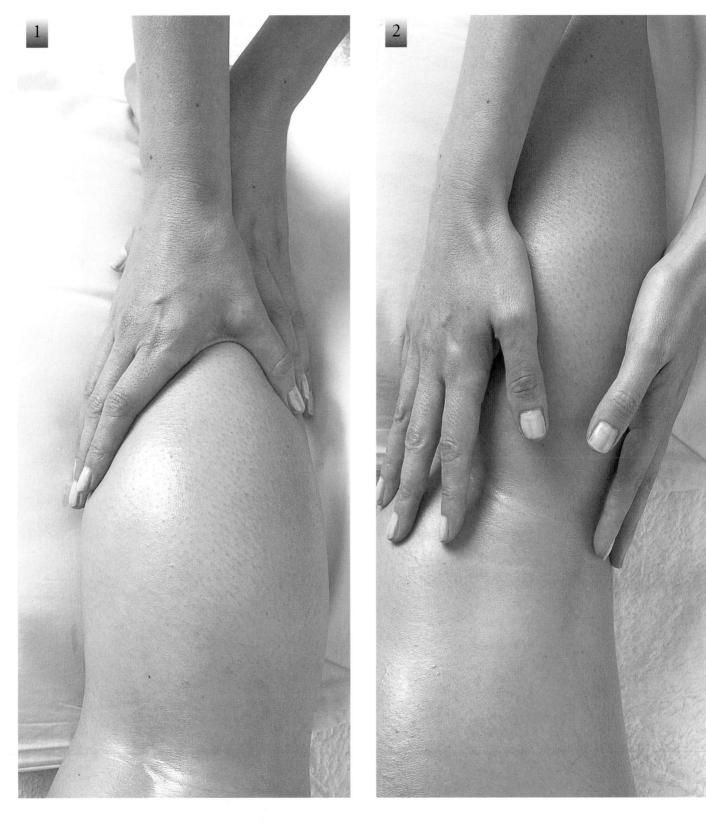

STEP 1. Now you will practice effleurage on the back of the leg. Place both hands palms down just above the ankle in a V-shape. Stroke firmly up the leg applying hardly any pressure to the back of the knee.

STEP 2. As your hands reach the top of the thigh separate them and allow them to glide gently back to your starting position.

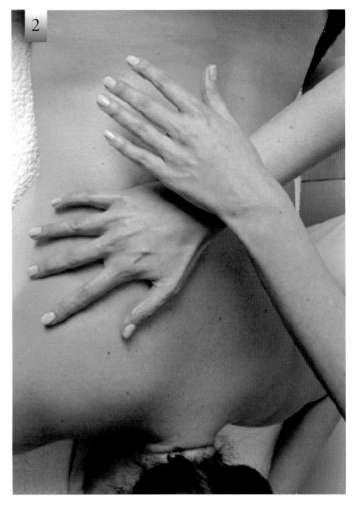

STEP 1. Effleurage may also be performed in a circular direction. Position yourself to one side of the receiver and place both hands palms downward on the opposite side of the body around the shoulder blade.

STEPS 2 - 3. Using the whole of the palms of the hands, make large stroking movements in a circular direction with one hand following the other down towards the buttocks and back up to the shoulders again. Your hands will cross over as you perform your circular movements. Make sure that you always keep contact with the receiver as you will have to lift one hand over the other.

You may perform the circular movements in either a clockwise or an anti-clockwise direction.

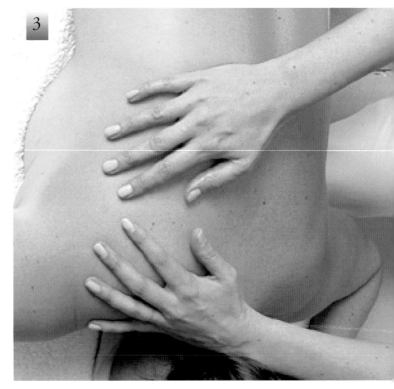

10

If an area needs to be thoroughly warmed up to prepare it for some deeper movements (e.g. the shoulder blade), or firm pressure is required then circular effleurage with one hand reinforcing the other may be performed. Place one hand flat on top of the other on one of the shoulder blades. Using the whole of the hand make large circular movements on and around the scapula.

THERAPEUTIC EFFECTS OF EFFLEURAGE

● A relationship of trust is established between you and the receiver.

● The receiver experiences a deep sense of relaxation.

● Slow effleurage is excellent for soothing the nerves and is highly beneficial for highly-strung or anxious individuals. Stress can be relieved and headaches and migraines dispelled. Blood pressure can be brought down significantly and patterns of insomnia can be broken. Slow effleurage is excellent after any sporting activity for eliminating waste products such as lactic acid and other deposits from the tissues. Recovery time can be greatly accelerated.

● Brisk effleurage is useful for stimulating the body. It improves the circulation and encourages the flow of lymph so that waste substances can be eliminated. Vigorous effleurage is particularly effective prior to any sporting event. When combined with other massage movements it can increase performance and agility and can prevent muscle strains from occurring.

REMEMBER

Never lose contact with the receiver

❖

Massage towards the heart with no pressure whatsoever on the downward stroke

❖

Ensure that your hands are relaxed and use the palmar surface

❖

Avoid any jerky movements – effleurage is always rhythmic and smooth

❖

Use more oil when treating a hairy person or you could create a rash

PETRISSAGE

Petrissage is derived from the word 'pétrir' which means to knead. There are several ways of performing petrissage and here it is divided into picking up, squeezing, rolling and wringing. This technique allows you to work deeply on the muscles and it is particularly effective when performed on fleshy areas such as the calves (shown here), hips, thighs and across the shoulders. This movement is suitable for every area of the body except the face.

PICKING UP

STEP 1. Place the hands palms flat down on the area to be treated. Grasp the muscle (not the skin) with both hands and then pick it up and pull it away as far as possible from the bone. Hold this position for a few seconds and then release the pressure, although your hands should still remain in contact with the receiver. Practice this movement on the back of the legs.

SQUEEZING

STEP 2. To perform this technique pick up the muscle as before and then gently squeeze it between your hands. This allows you to 'squeeze' out any toxins that have accumulated from the deeper tissues.

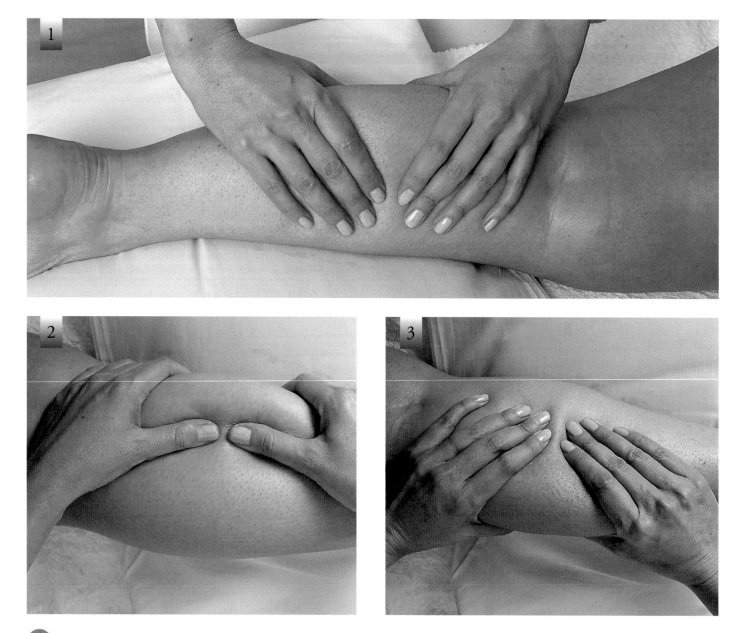

ROLLING

STEP 3. Muscles may be rolled in both directions – the thumbs can roll the muscle towards the fingers or the fingers may roll the muscle towards the thumbs. Place both hands flat onto the area to be treated and lift and roll the muscle in both directions. (2, 3)

WRINGING

STEP 4. For a really deep effect try wringing. Once again this movement is performed on the large muscle groups. The muscle is picked up between the thumb and fingers, each hand working alternately, pulled towards you and 'wrung' out as if you are wringing out a towel or chamois leather.

Wringing may also be done slowly and gently around the shoulder area.

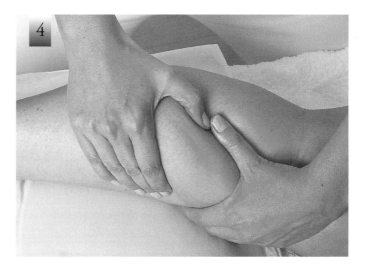

THERAPEUTIC EFFECTS OF PETRISSAGE

● An increased blood supply is brought to the area being treated, bringing fresh nutrients to the muscles.

● The deeper tissues are cleansed of any accumulated toxins.

● Fatty deposits are broken down.

● Muscle tone is improved.

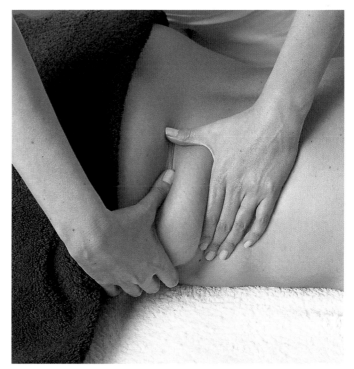

REMEMBER

Make sure that you are grasping the whole of the muscle – not just the skin

❖

Use the whole of your hand and NOT just the fingers and thumbs otherwise you will pinch and cause discomfort to the receiver

Be careful to avoid painful pinching when using petrissage techniques.

FRICTION

To perform friction, the balls of the thumbs are usually employed. However, the fingertips and knuckles can also be used, as well as the elbows. This technique is an excellent way of finding and breaking down knots and nodules which can build up, particularly around the shoulder blades and on either side of the spine. You will perfect this technique on the back.

STEP 1. Place the pads of your thumbs in the dimples at the base of the spine. Keep your arms straight and slowly lean forward so that you are using your body weight to penetrate into the deeper tissues. Press for a few seconds whilst rotating your thumbs then gradually release the pressure and move your thumbs slightly further up the back. Repeat this pressure until you reach the base of the neck.

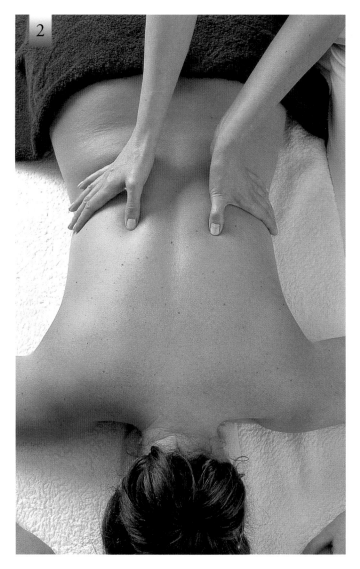

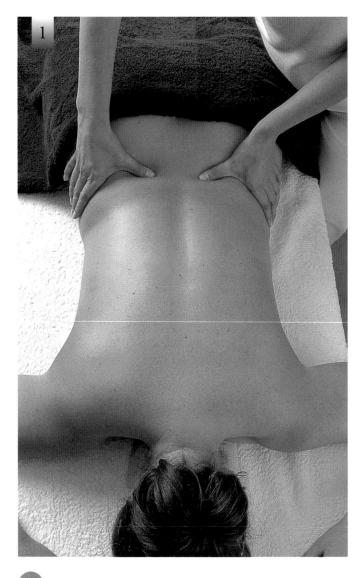

STEP 2. To perform continuous circular friction, assume the same position as before. Perform small deep, outward circular movements with the balls of your thumbs, pulling the muscle away from the spine. Your thumbs should ache by the time you reach the base of the neck. If you find a 'knotty' area then place one thumb on top of the other and perform some circular friction over it.

STEP 3. The knuckles may also be employed for breaking down knots and nodules. Curl your hands into fists and use your knuckles in a circular motion.

3

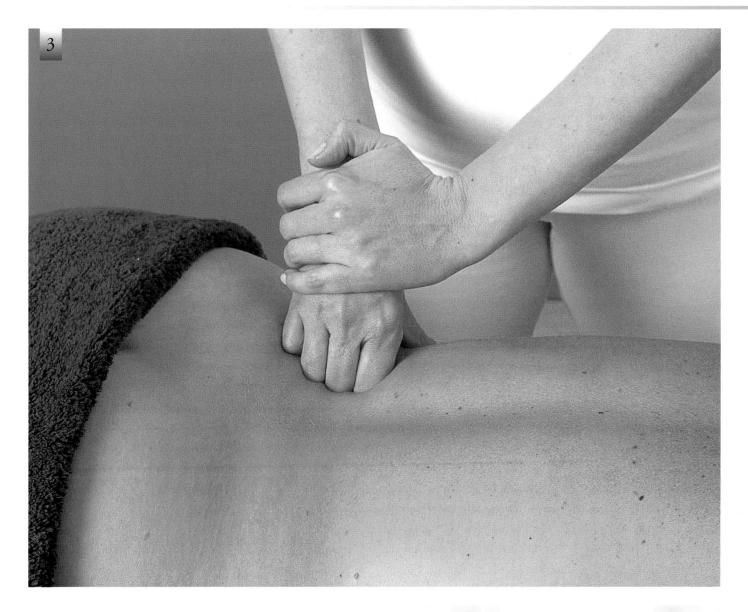

THERAPEUTIC EFFECTS OF FRICTION

● Friction breaks down knots and nodules.

● Waste products are eliminated.

● Fatty deposits are broken down.

● Old scar tissue may be broken down.

● Pain can be relieved.

● Joints can be loosened.

REMEMBER

Make sure that you are working on the
deeper muscles and not just the skin

❖

Do not poke and prod. Press slowly
into the tissues, gradually working
deeper and deeper

❖

Use the pads of the thumbs and not the
tips to avoid digging the nails in

P E R C U S S I O N   M O V E M E N T S / T A P O T E M E N T

Tapotement consists of a variety of movements in which the muscles are stimulated using various parts of the hands such as the edge of the hand, the palms or even the fists. Percussion movements are only performed on fleshy, muscular areas – never on bony areas.

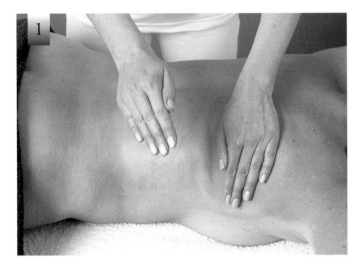

CUPPING
Cupping is also sometimes referred to as a clapping. Form a hollow curve with your fingers and thumbs and bring your cupped hands down on to the body in quick succession. (1)

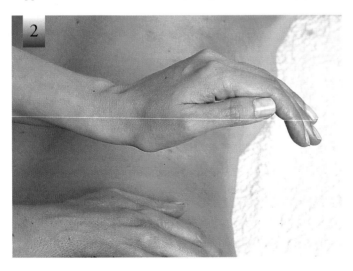

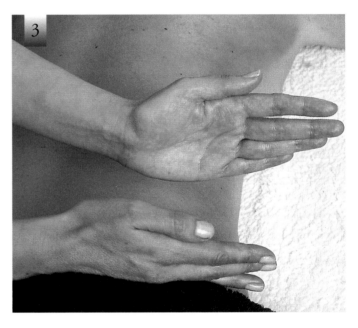

You should hear a hollow sound (NOT a slapping sound) as your cupped hands create a vacuum, trapping air against the skin and then releasing it. When properly applied cupping will not hurt. (2)

THERAPEUTIC EFFECTS OF TAPOTEMENT

● Circulation improves as blood is drawn to the surface.

● Muscle tone is induced.

● Fatty deposits are reduced.

● Cupping can help to loosen mucus in the lungs.

● Percussion movements are stimulating and highly beneficial prior to sporting activities.

HACKING
This technique is performed with the outer edge of the hands. Make sure that you keep the wrists very loose. Hold your hands over the body, thumbs uppermost with the palms facing each other. Now flick your hands rhythmically up and down in quick succession. Your movements should be light and bouncy and NOT sharp and heavy like a karate chop. (3)

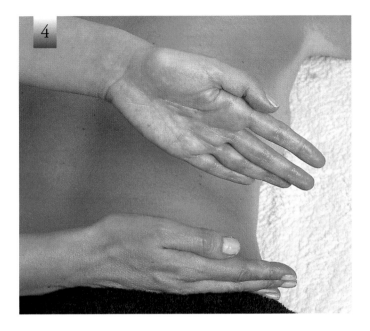

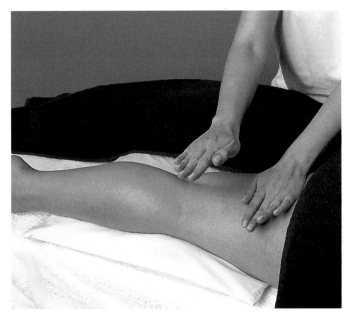

Make sure your hands are cupped rather than flat to avoid 'smacking' the receiver

FLICKING

This is a lighter version of hacking. The difference between these two movements is that in flicking only the sides of the little fingers are used and not the edge of the hand. Flicking has a much softer effect. (4)

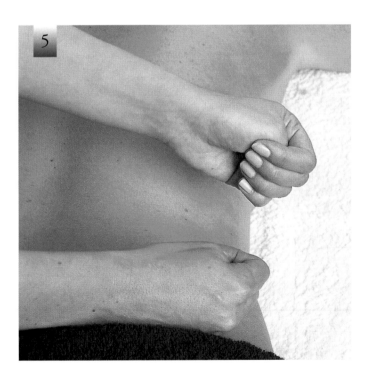

POUNDING

To perform pounding, clench your fists lightly and apply them to the body alternately in quick succession. (5)

REMEMBER

Do not perform over bony areas e.g. shins. Percussion movements should only be used on fleshy muscular areas

❖

Do not perform over sensitive areas e.g. back of the knee, neck, bruises, broken veins etc

❖

When cupping, make sure your hands are cupped and NOT flat to avoid smacking

❖

Keep the wrists loose and your movements light and bouncy to avoid causing discomfort to the receiver

E X E R C I S E S   F O R   Y O U R   H A N D S

The following exercises will help you improve the flexibility and strength of your hands as well as helping to heighten your sensitivity.

Hold a small rubber ball in one hand and repeatedly squeeze and relax your fingers around the ball. This exercise will help to build up strength in your hands. (1)

To keep the wrists supple, circle both wrists in a clockwise and anti-clockwise direction. (2)

Relax your hands and bend each joint to slowly close each hand and make a fist with the thumb outside the fingers.(3)

Now throw your fingers out so that they are extended and separated as far as possible.(4)

Practice the percussion movements – cupping, hacking, flicking and pounding - on a cushion to build up speed and expertise.(5)

To enhance sensitivity place a coin under a magazine, close your eyes and try to 'sense' where the coin is. If you find this too difficult, place the coin under a few sheets of paper to begin with and then gradually increase the thickness. You can also try this exercise placing a piece of hair under a sheet of paper. When you find this easy then increase the density of the barrier.

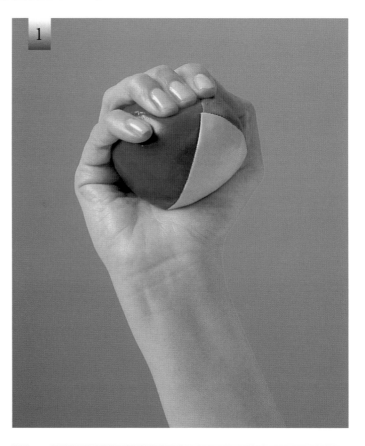

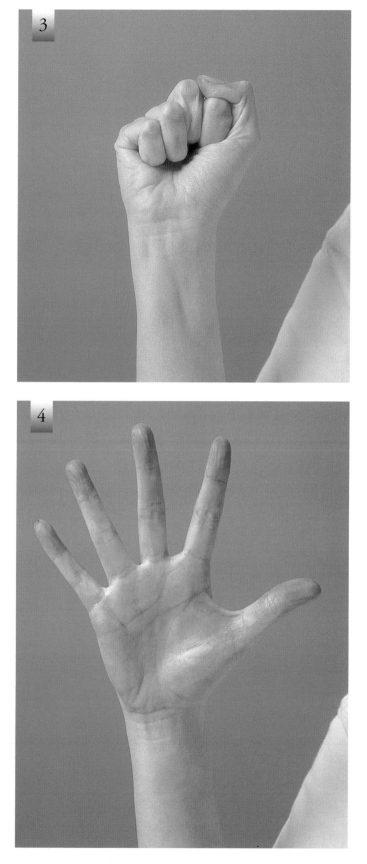

Close and open each hand to increase flexibility and strength.

Practise percussion movements on a cushion to increase speed and expertise.

therapeutic
Massage Sequence

This step-by-step section will enable you to carry out a complete full body therapeutic massage on your family and friends. A complete treatment will probably take you about one and a half hours, although if time is limited then the areas most in need of treatment should be selected.

Before embarking on the massage routine ensure that you have created the right environment and that the receiver is not suffering from a problem which is contra-indicated to massage (see contra-indications). If you are in any doubt seek the advice of the doctor or a professional massage therapist.

The receiver should lie on his/her front with one pillow placed under the feet, to prevent friction of the toes, and one under the head and shoulders. If you are fortunate enough to have a massage couch then the face can rest on a face hole ring in the breathing hole. Some people (particularly well-endowed women) find it comfortable to have a pillow under the breast area. The arms should be placed at the sides or hung over the edge of the massage couch. Completely cover the receiver with towels to preserve modesty and to make the receiver feel warm and secure.

BENEFITS OF LEG MASSAGE

- Improves the circulation and helps to prevent and improve varicose veins.
- Reduces swelling and puffiness in the legs and ankles.
- Alleviates tightness and cramp.
- Helps to reduce cellulite and break down fatty deposits.
- Cleanses waste products such as lactic acid from the tissues after exercise.
- Improves muscle tone.
- Reduces muscle fatigue.
- Loosens up the joints and helps arthritis and other musculo-skeletal problems.
- Alleviates strain on the lower back.
- Helpful as a prelude to sporting activities.

BACK OF THE BODY

LEG MASSAGE

STEP 1 – tuning in
Lower the hands gently down onto the leg to be treated and take a few deep breaths allowing any tension to be released.

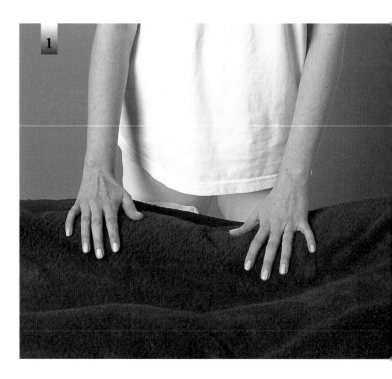

WHEN TO EXERCISE CAUTION

- If there is thrombo-phlebitis do NOT massage. The clot could move, resulting in death.
- If there is an infectious skin condition e.g. scabies or chicken pox, never massage.
- Avoid inflamed or swollen areas (e.g. a sprain or a burn). You can massage above and below the area.
- Avoid recent scars.
- Take care over varicose veins – use only gentle effleurage over them.

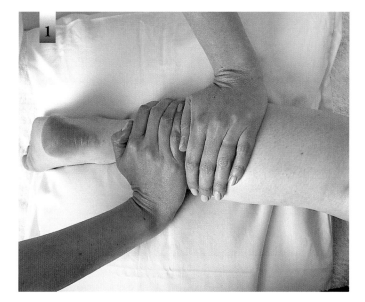

Massage techniques are exactly the same for either leg. For clarity of illustration, techniques have been performed on both legs.

STEP 1 – effleurage the calf

Place cupped hands over the back of the ankle, one hand above the other, and stroke up the calf until you reach the back of the knee. Allow your hands to glide gently back down the sides of the calf.

STEP 2 – effleurage the leg

Begin to apply the oil to the whole leg. Place your hands in a V-Shape with one hand in front of the other over the heel.

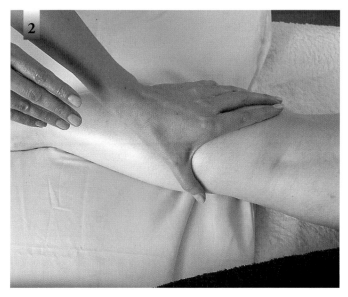

Effleurage the entire leg, applying firm pressure as you work up the leg. Do not, however, apply pressure to the back of the knee since this is a very delicate and sensitive area. As your hands reach the top of the thigh, allow them to separate and glide back down to your starting point with a feather light touch. Repeat this movement until you feel the leg begin to warm and the muscles softening.

Alternatively, place both hands over the back of the ankle and effleurage with one hand up to the back of the knee.

As your first hand lifts off, begin to effleurage with your other hand. Repeat this movement with one hand following behind the other. Stroke slowly for a relaxing treatment or briskly for a stimulating effect. (3)

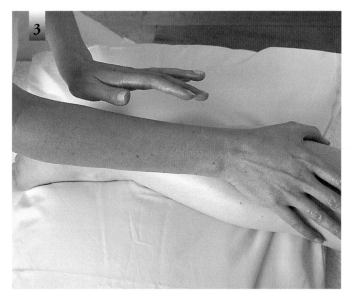

31

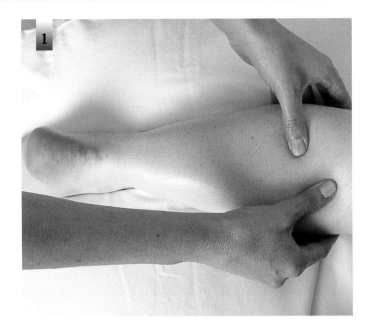

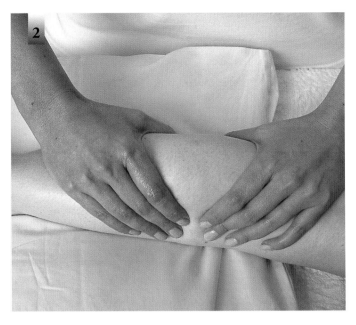

STEP 4 – gentle friction on the calf

Place both thumbs just above the heel and make small outward circular movements using your thumbs alternately. Glide gently back down to the ankle with no pressure. This movement helps to decongest the calf and helps to prepare it for some deeper work. (1)

STEP 5 – pick up and squeeze the calf

Working from the side place both hands flat down on the calf muscle and gently pick up and squeeze the muscles away from the bone. Remember to use your whole hand so that you avoid pinching with your thumbs and fingers. Imagine that you are squeezing out any accumulated toxins from the deeper tissues. (2)

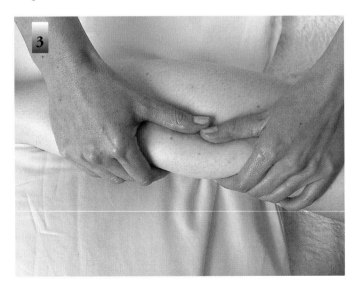

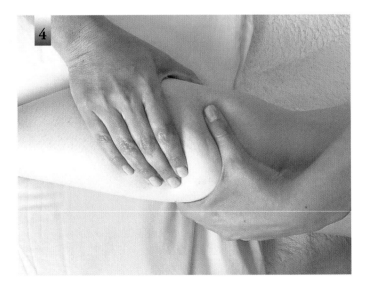

STEP 6 – pick up and roll the calf

Working from the same position, use the thumbs to pick up and roll the muscle away from you towards your fingers. Then lift and roll the muscle towards your thumbs. These movements will bring an increased blood supply and fresh nutrients to the muscles. (3)

STEP 7 – wring the calf

For a really detoxifying effect, use alternate hands to pull the muscle towards you as if you are wringing out a towel. (4)

STEP 8 – effleurage the leg
Stroke the entire leg again to move any waste deposits that have
been released towards the groin area so that they can be
eliminated.(1)

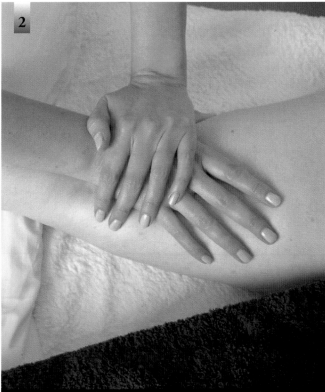

STEP 9 – effleurage the thigh
Stroke up the thigh from the knee to the groin using firm pressure
on the way up and a feather light touch on the return. For extra
depth apply pressure with the heel of your hands. These
movements prepare the thigh for the deeper techniques.(2)

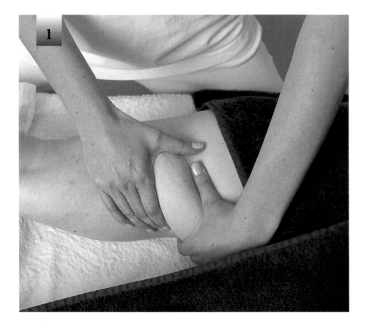

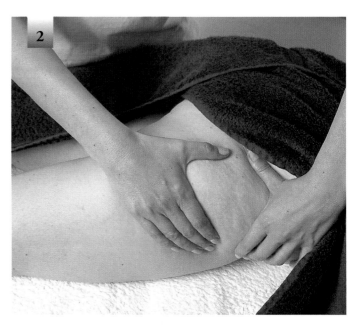

STEP 10 – knead the thigh
Wring the inner thigh using gentle pressure, as this is a delicate area. (1)

Wring the outer thigh using a much firmer and stronger action. Pay particular attention to any fatty deposits and cellulite that have accumulated in the thighs. (2)

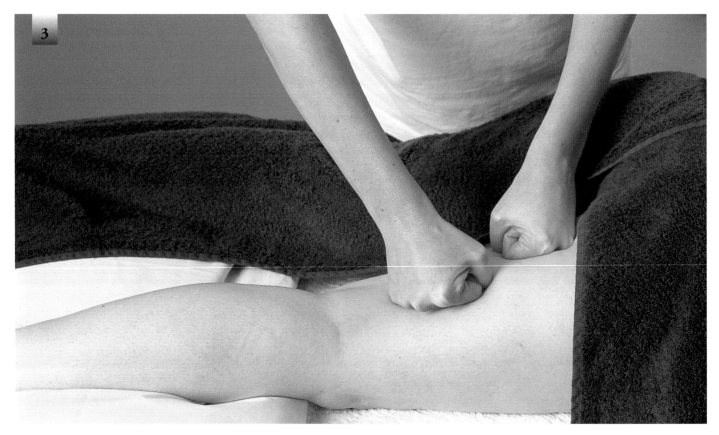

STEP 11 – knuckle the thigh
Make your hands into fists and use your knuckles in a circular direction to further break down fatty deposits. (3)

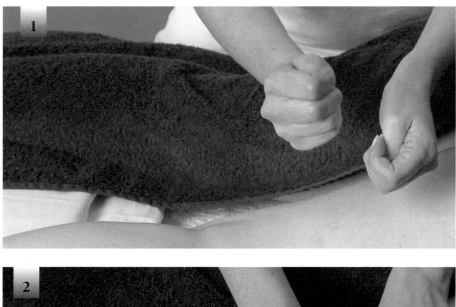

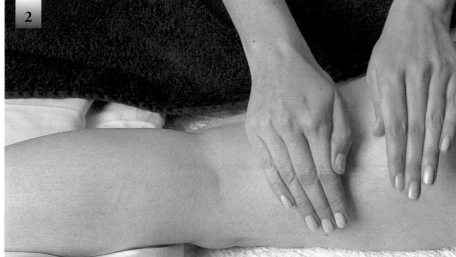

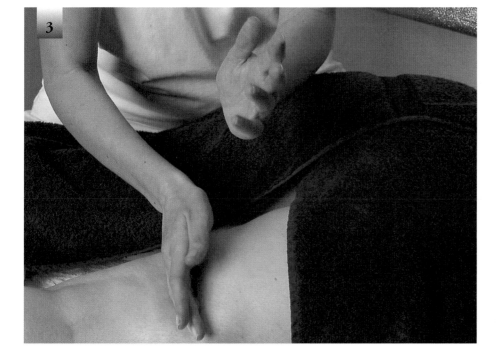

STEP 12 – pound the thigh
Still with your fists lightly clenched, pound the thighs using your fists alternately in quick succession.(1)

STEP 13 – cup the leg
Form a hollow curve with your fingers and thumbs and bring your cupped hands down onto the leg in quick succession. You should hear a hollow sound as you cup the whole of the back of the leg, avoiding the delicate area at the back of the knee.(2)

STEP 14 – hack the leg
Using the outer edge of your hands, flick your hands rhythmically up and down. Use your hands alternately working very quickly up and down the leg. Remember to keep your wrists very loose and keep your movements light and bouncy. (3)

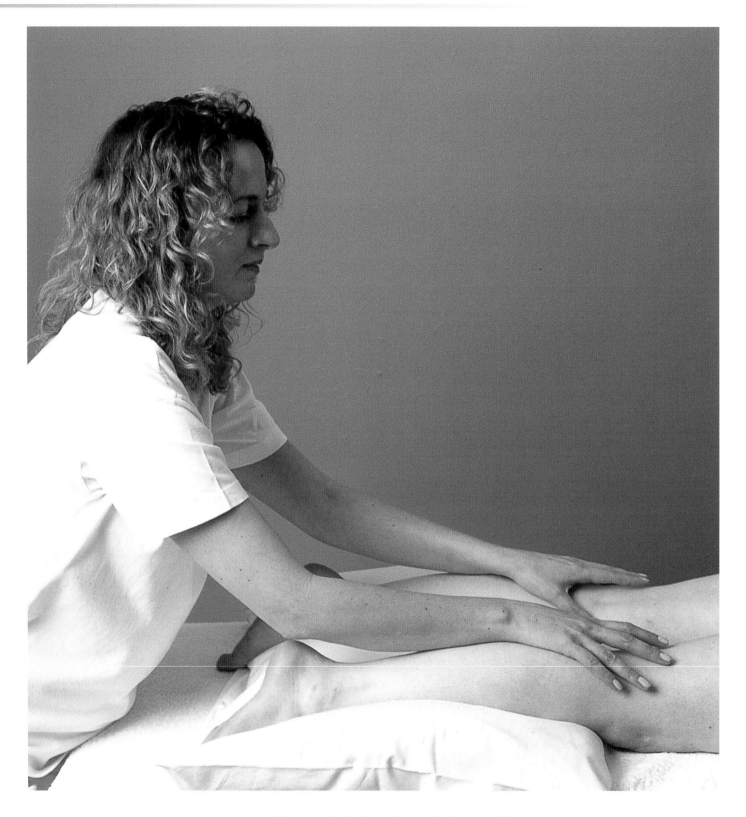

STEP 15 – the final touch – gentle fingertip effleurage
Stroke gently down both legs from the top of the thigh to the ankle using just your fingertips to completely relax the legs. Allow your hands to come to rest on the heels and then lift them slowly and gently away. Repeat on the other leg.

BACK AND SHOULDER MASSAGE

BENEFITS OF BACK MASSAGE
● The nervous system benefits enormously. Stress levels are lowered and a deep sense of relaxation is induced.
● Insomnia is relieved.
● Tense muscles are relaxed and backache and shoulder problems are relieved.
● Bronchial problems such as asthma improve as breathing deepens as massaging the upper back decongests the lungs.
● Reduces fatty deposits.
● Induces muscle tone.
● Improves circulation, strengthens the heart and reduces blood pressure.
● Helps to eliminate waste products from the body.

WHEN TO EXERCISE CAUTION
● If there is an infectious skin condition e.g. measles or impetigo, do not massage.
● Avoid recent scars.
● If there is a lump or bump a doctor should check it out.
● Avoid swollen or inflamed areas.
● If back pain is severe, a doctor or a fully qualified osteopath should be consulted.

STEP 1 – tuning in
Place both hands on the back and take a few deep breaths as you feel the tension melting away. (1)

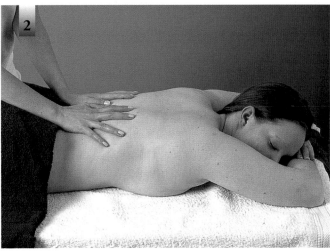

STEP 2 – effleurage
Position yourself to the side of the receiver, draw back the towel and oil the back using stroking movements. Place both hands palms down, one either side of the spine, fingers pointing upwards on the lower back. (2)

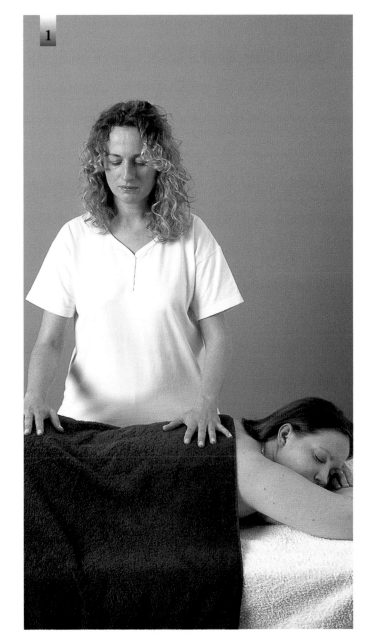

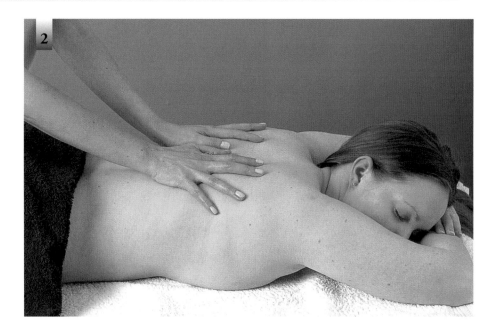

2

Stroke firmly up the back and as your hands reach the top of the back, spread them outwards across the shoulders.

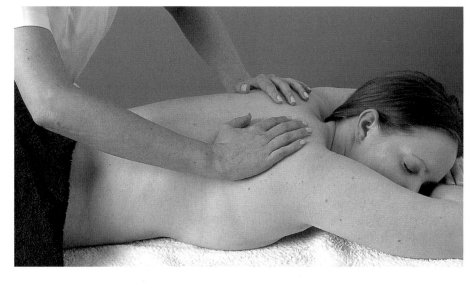

Then allow them to glide back to your starting point with no pressure. If the receiver requires firmer pressure then lean into the movement so that your whole body becomes involved.

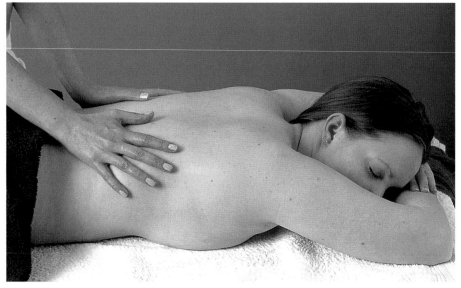

Repeat your effleurage movements several times to completely relax the receiver.

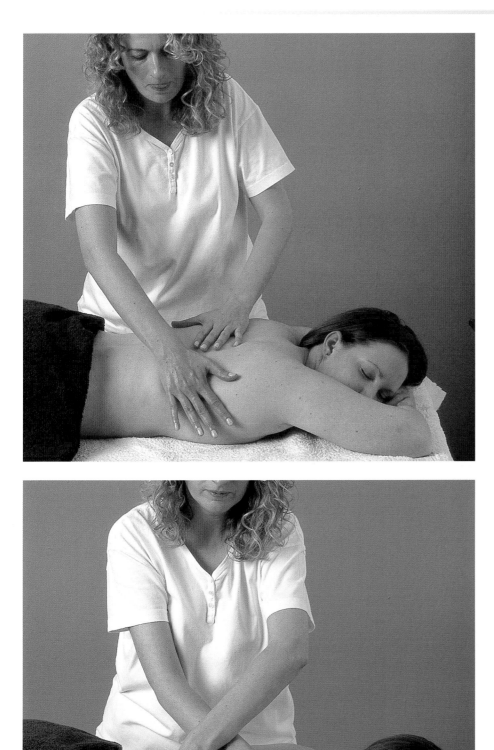

STEP 3 – circular effleurage
Still working from the side, place both hands palms down on the opposite side of the upper back with one hand slightly higher than the other.

Make large stroking movements in a circular direction one hand following the other working down towards the buttocks and back up again. Repeat on the other side of the back.

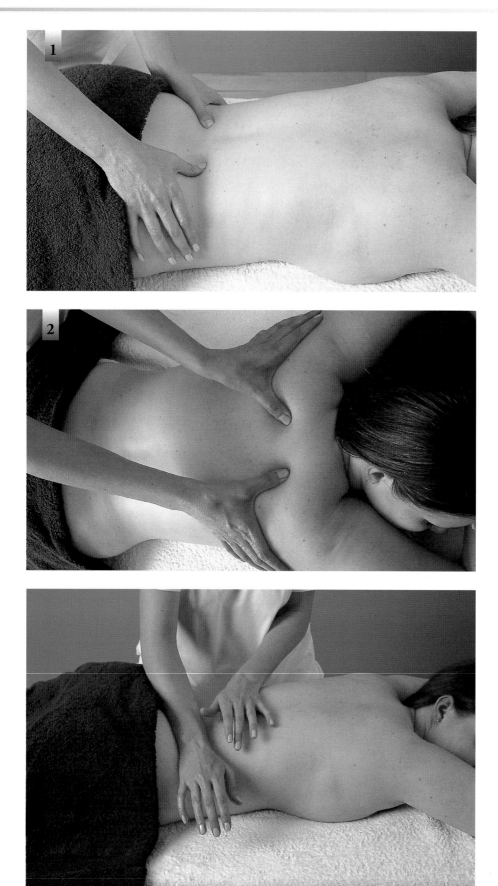

STEP 4 – friction on the spinal muscles
Place the balls of the thumbs in the two dimples that are usually visible at the base of the spine. (1,2)

Using small, deep, outward circular movements work up towards the neck. Try to maintain the same distance between your thumbs as you proceed up the spinal muscles. If you find any knots and nodules place one thumb on top of the other and perform circular friction over the area pressing in as far as is comfortable for the receiver. On reaching the neck, allow your hands to glide back using no pressure.

STEP 5 – heel of hand stroke down the sides of the back
This technique allows you to loosen up the back muscles further and to drain away any toxins released by the friction. Place both hands palms downward on the opposite side of the spine but not directly on the spine. Using alternate heels of the hands, one closely following the other, work up and down the back pushing downwards. Start the movement with the heel of your hand and follow it through with your forearm. Repeat these movements on the other side of the back.

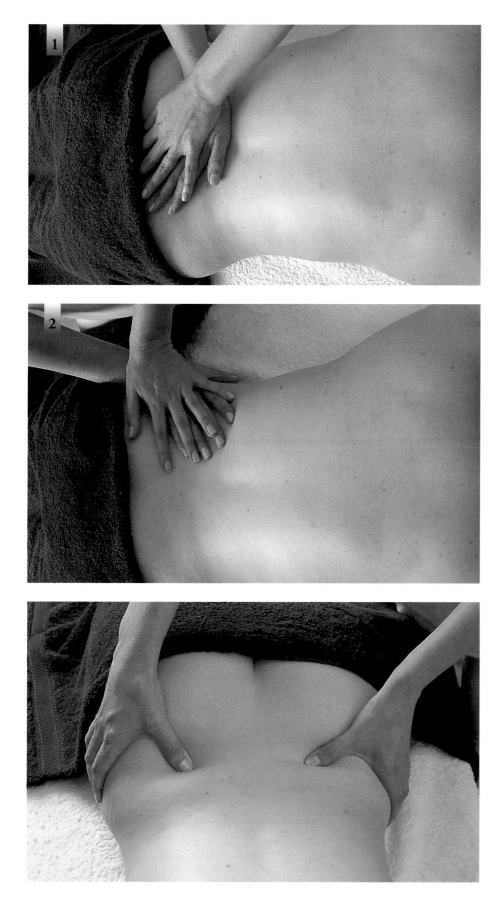

STEP 6 – effleurage the lower back and buttock area
Place one hand flat on top of your other hand on one of the buttocks. Make large figure of eight movements, circling over one buttock and then over the other. (1,2)

STEP 7 – friction the top of the pelvis
Locate the dimples at the base of the spine and, using the pads of your thumbs, make deep circular friction movements across the top of the pelvis.

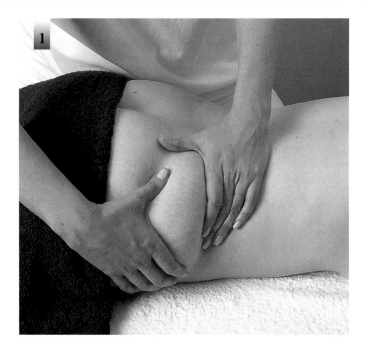

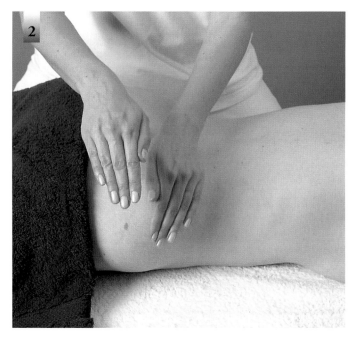

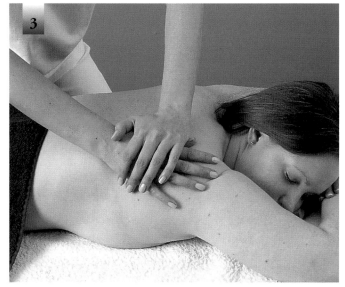

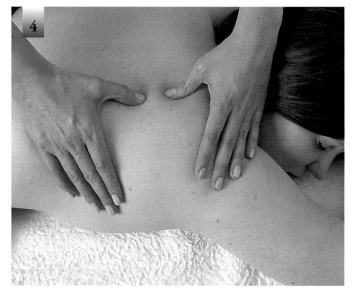

STEP 8 – petrissage the buttocks and waist
Wring the entire buttock and waist area with alternate hands. There is usually plenty of flesh in this area. (1)

STEP 9 – cup the buttocks and waist area
Percussion movements help to improve tone in this area. Cup the buttocks and waist thoroughly and then make loose fists to perform pounding. Hacking and pounding and flicking can also be performed. (2)

STEP 10 – effleurage the shoulders
Effleurage up towards the shoulders bringing the towel up with you to cover up the buttocks and lower back. To warm and loosen the shoulders, place one hand flat on top of the other and perform circular effleurage on and around the shoulder blade (3)

STEP 11 – friction around the shoulder blade
You may either work on the scapula nearest you or, if you find it more comfortable, work on the scapula opposite you. Using the balls of your thumbs apply deep, circular frictions all around the rim of the shoulder blade. You will find lots of knots in this area, which need to be broken down with friction movements. Then work on the other shoulder blade.(4)

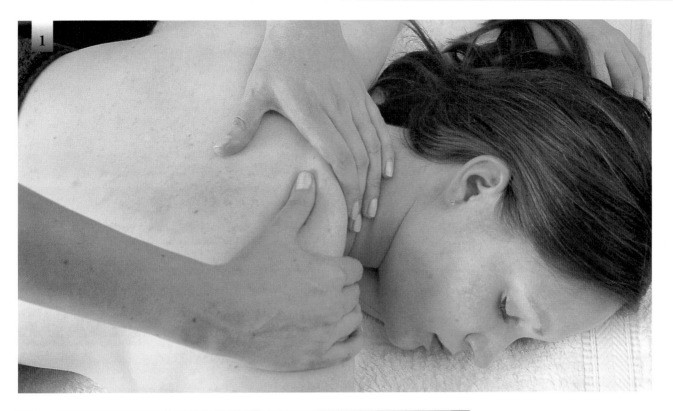

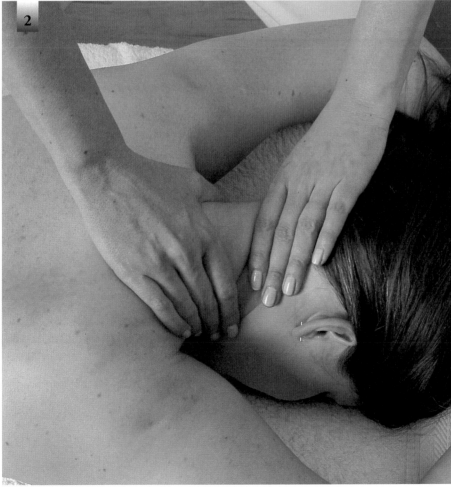

STEP 12 – petrissage the shoulders
To remove the remaining tension, wring the top of both shoulders picking up as much muscle as you can, using alternate hands. Do this slowly and gently.(1)

STEP 13 – pick up the neck
If you are working on a couch it is easy to pick up the neck as the receiver can use the face hole. If not then place a small rolled up towel or pillow under the head and ask him/her to place their hands under the forehead to straighten out the back of the neck. Pick up and squeeze the muscles slowly and gently to disperse any tightness in the neck. This is an invaluable area to work on if the receiver suffers with headaches or migraine.(2)

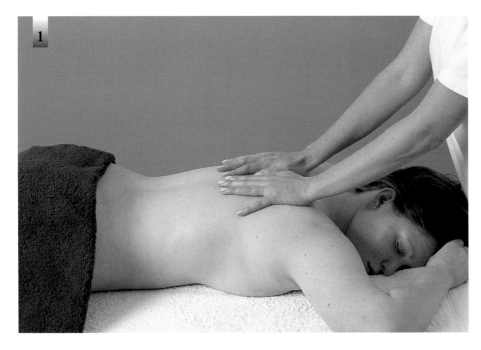

STEP 14 – effleurage the whole back
Position yourself at the receiver's head and place your hands on the top of the shoulders. Stroke slowly down the back and over the buttocks. Allow your hands to glide back with a feather light touch. (1)

STEP 15 – the final touch – fingertip stroking
Using just your fingertips so that you are hardly touching the skin, stroke very slowly and lightly down either side of the spine. As they reach the low back gently lift them off and return them to the neck area. With each stroke use lighter and lighter pressure. (2)

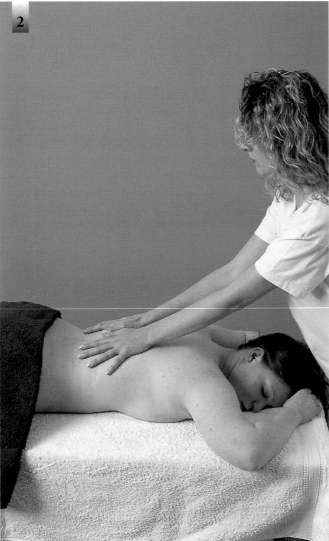

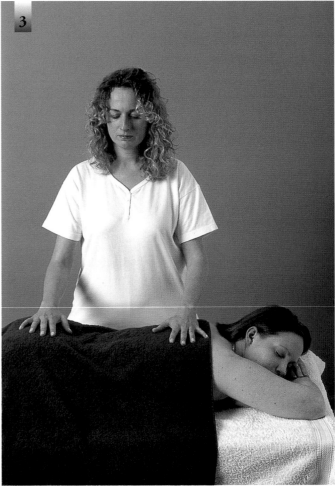

Completely cover the whole back and finally let your hands rest intuitively on the back. (3)

FRONT OF THE BODY

FOOT MASSAGE

Ask the receiver to turn over. Place a pillow/cushion under the head and one under the knees for support to take the pressure off the low back. Only cover the foot that you intend to work on first.

BENEFITS OF FOOT MASSAGE
● Improves the circulation.
● Reduces puffiness and swelling particularly around the ankles.
● Alleviates and prevents cramp.
● Reduces stiffness and improves flexibility in the ankle and toe joints.
● Gives a treatment to the whole of the body. According to reflexology, all the organs and parts of the body are found in miniature in the feet.
● Eliminates toxins.

WHEN TO EXERCISE CAUTION
● If there is an infectious condition such as athlete's foot or a verruca avoid the area so that you do not spread it. Neat pure essential oils of tea tree or lemon may be applied using a cotton bud to the affected area.
● Take care over corns and blisters – if they are painful avoid them.
● Do not massage swollen or inflamed joints (e.g. gout in the big toe) or you may cause pain and further inflammation.
● Avoid recent scars. Old scar tissue should be frictioned.
● Do not use heavy pressure on varicose veins or where the skin is thin or bruises easily (e.g. a diabetic).

STEP 1 – tuning in
To tune in uncover one foot and clasp it very gently between your hands. Close your eyes and take a few deep breaths allowing the tension to flow out of the body. (1)

STEP 2 – effleurage the foot
Always make sure that you only use a minute amount of oil when treating the feet. Too much oil makes it difficult for you to hold the foot properly. Also pick up the foot firmly to avoid tickling the receiver. Using both hands stroke up the entire foot firmly from the tips of the toes to the top of the foot, covering the top, sides and sole of the foot. As you reach the ankle glide around it and back again with no pressure. (2)

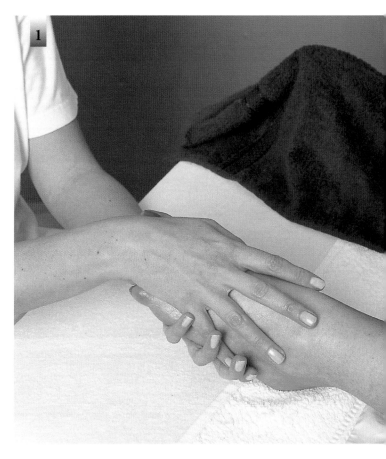

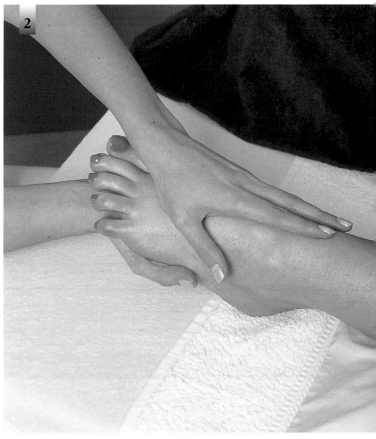

STEP 3 – metatarsal kneading
Wrap one hand around the foot, fingers on the top of the foot, thumb on the sole. Make a fist with your other hand and place it on the fleshy area of the ball of the foot. Using a circular action, work from the ball of the foot to the heel. These movements help to soften the tissues and loosen up the sole of the foot.

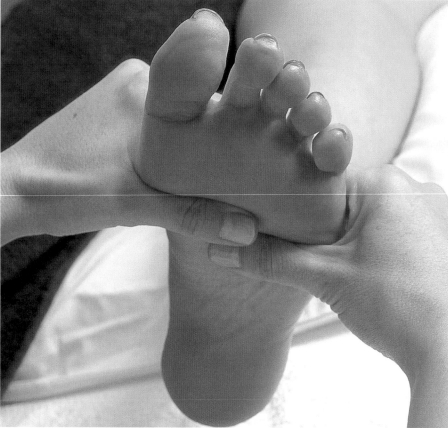

STEP 4 – spread the foot
Place your thumbs flat down on the sole of the foot, fingers on top. One thumb needs to be slightly higher than the other. Pull the thumbs away from each other towards the edge of the foot and allow them to glide back towards each other. Repeat these movements from the base of the toes to the heel and then back again. Feel that you are opening out the foot.

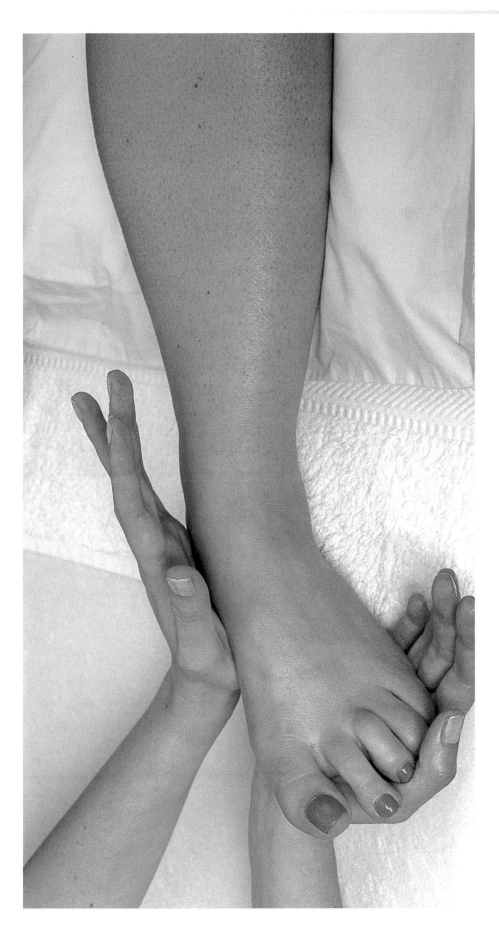

STEP 5 – stroke the inside of the foot
This movement not only allows the foot
to relax further but it also loosens up the
spine, as according to foot reflexology
the spine is located on the inner aspect of
the foot. Cup the heel of the foot in one
hand and with the heel of your other
hand stroke firmly down the inside of the
foot, working from the big toe towards
the heel.

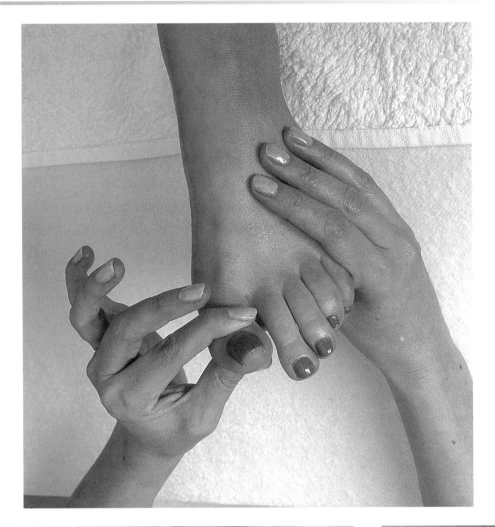

STEP 6 – toes
Massage the joints of the toes, both top and bottom, using small circular friction movements to loosen them

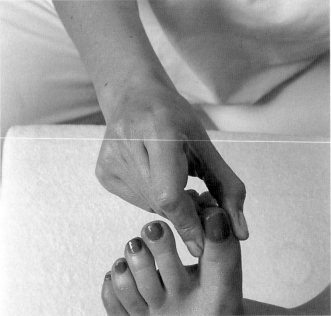

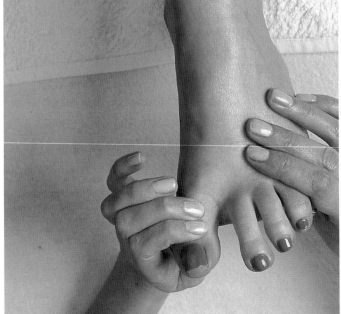

Then with your thumb and index finger, slowly stretch each toe individually.

Then rotate each one both clockwise and anti-clockwise. These movements will greatly improve the flexibility of the toes.

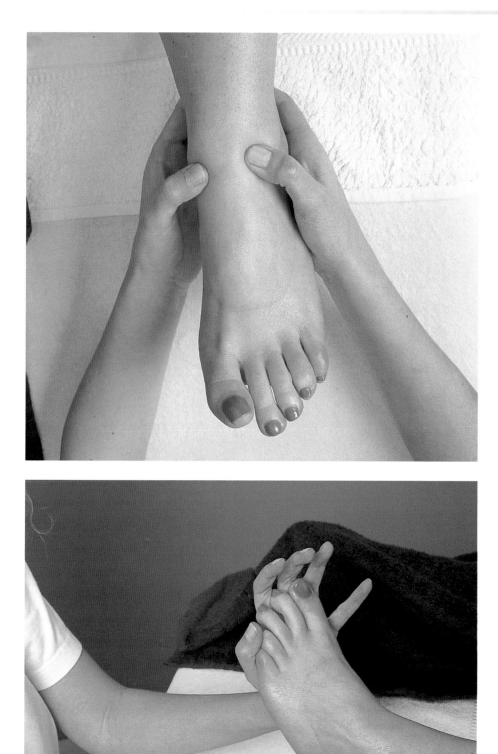

STEP 7 – ankle loosening
Massage all around the ankle joint with both thumbs using small, deep circular friction movements. If you encounter any 'gritty' areas then work deeply into the area to break down old scar tissue and eliminate waste deposits.

STEP 8 – ankle rotation
Supporting the heel of the foot with one hand, gently grasp the top of the foot with your other hand. Slowly rotate the ankle several times in one direction and then in the other to mobilise the ankle. This technique should be performed with caution if there is a problem with the Achilles tendon.

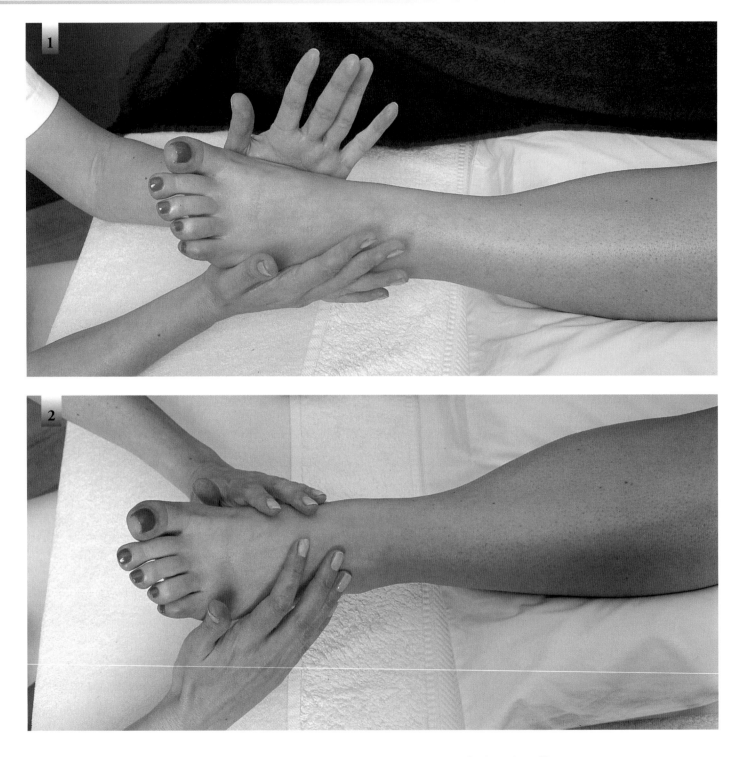

STEP 9 – foot vibrations

Place the palms of your hands one either side of the foot. One hand needs to be slightly higher than the other. Move them alternately and rapidly up and down the sides of the foot. Work along the edges of the foot from the heel to the toes and back again. This movement is excellent for stimulating the circulation, releasing tension and increasing the mobility of the foot. (1 & 2)

STEP 10 – the final touch – effleurage

Using just the fingertips of both hands, stroke the foot slowly and gently from the toes, around the anklebones and back again. Then clasp the foot between both of your hands and squeeze very gently.

MASSAGE OF THE FRONT OF THE LEG

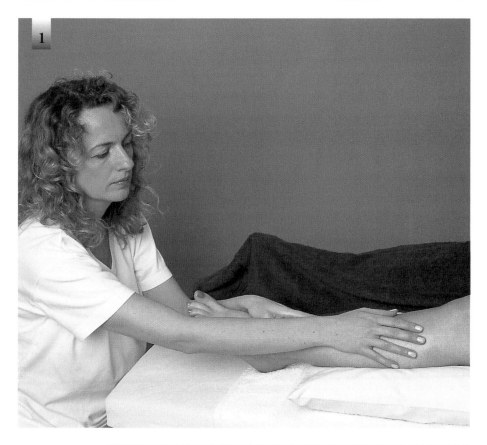

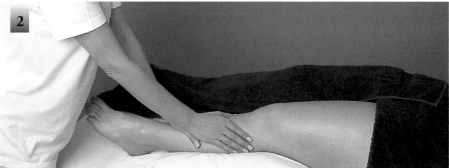

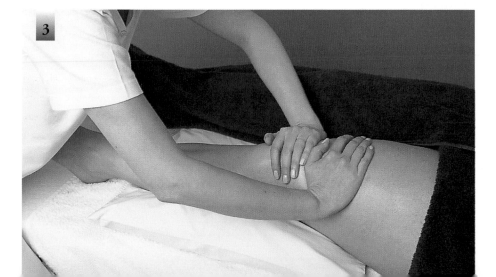

● In cases of thrombo-phlebitis never massage since the clot could move and cause death.

● Take care over advanced varicose veins. Use only GENTLE effleurage – firm massage could cause further inflammation and pain.

● Avoid recent scar tissue.

● Never massage DIRECTLY over an inflamed or swollen area of the leg e.g. bursitis (housemaid's knee). Massage is beneficial above and below the affected area.

● Always check out any suspicious lumps, swellings, moles etc.

● Where there is an infectious skin condition such as scabies, never massage.

● Take special care on the front of the lower leg since this is a very delicate, somewhat bony, area. The elderly, diabetics and individuals on certain medications such as steroids and blood thinning drugs may have thin skin and be susceptible to bruising.

STEP 1 – tuning in
To tune in place both hands on the front of the leg and take a few deep breaths. (1)

STEP 2 – effleurage the leg
Stroke firmly up the leg from the ankle to the top of the thigh and glide gently back down the sides. Ensure that you use only light pressure over the thigh, moulding your hands to the contours of the leg. You may effleurage with your hands in a V-shape with one hand in front of the other. (2)

Alternately effleurage with cupped hands, one hand above the other. (3)

51

STEP 3 – effleurage the lower leg
Place both hands in a V-shape over the
front of the ankle. Effleurage with one
hand up the front of the leg.

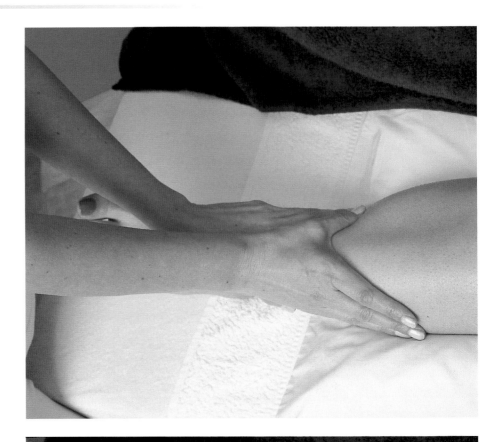

As your first hand reaches the knee, lift it
off and begin to effleurage with your
other hand. Take great care over this area
of the leg, as it is a bony and often very
sensitive area particularly where the skin
is thin.

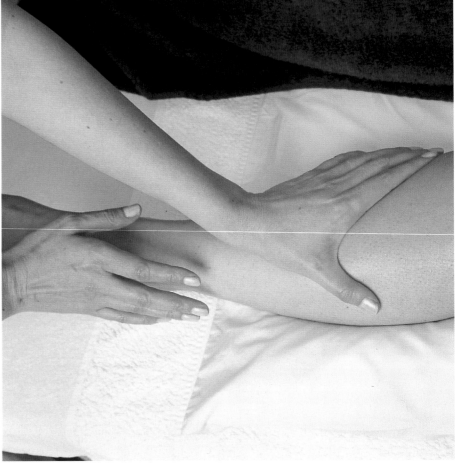

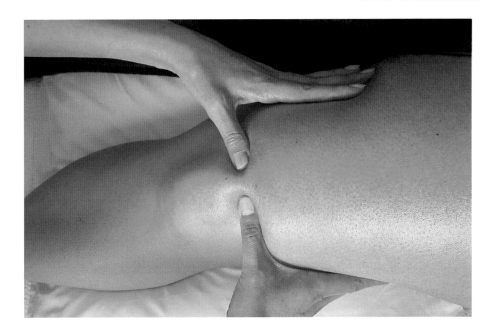

STEP 4 – thumb circling the kneecap
Place both thumbs just below the knee joint. Glide gently around the knee, one thumb on either side, until they meet at the top.

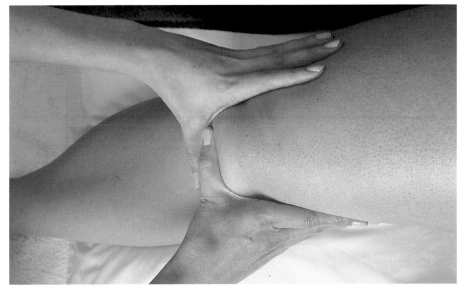

Then do another circle, allowing them to meet underneath the knee.

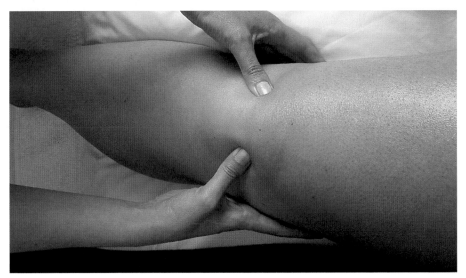

STEP 5 – loosening the patella (kneecap)
Use the pads of the thumbs to work all around the kneecap using small circular friction movements. This technique is excellent for arthritis of the knee or for breaking down old scar tissue and gives more mobility to the joint. Remember that if the knee is inflamed then do not massage DIRECTLY onto it. Work the muscles above and below the area to gently disperse any fluid.

STEP 6 – effleurage the thigh
Place your hands just above the knee and firmly effleurage the front of the thigh. For extra pressure, stroke with the heels of the hands. Glide your hands gently back.

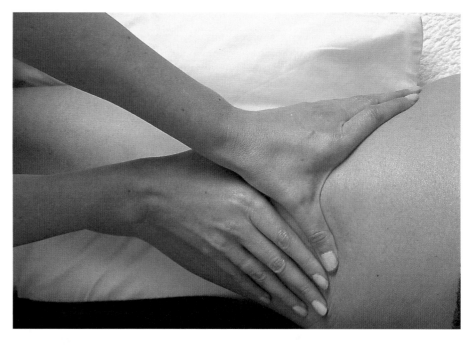

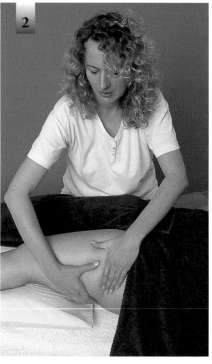

STEP 7 – petrissage the thigh
Place the hands flat down on the thigh and wring the muscles with alternate hands. Work gently on the inner thigh muscles, which are sensitive. (1)

As you petrissage the outer thigh, work from the opposite side of the receiver for maximum comfort. These movements allow you to bring the deeper toxins to the surface and to break down and eliminate fatty deposits. Muscle tone, as well as the appearance of the thighs, should greatly improve over a period of time. (2)

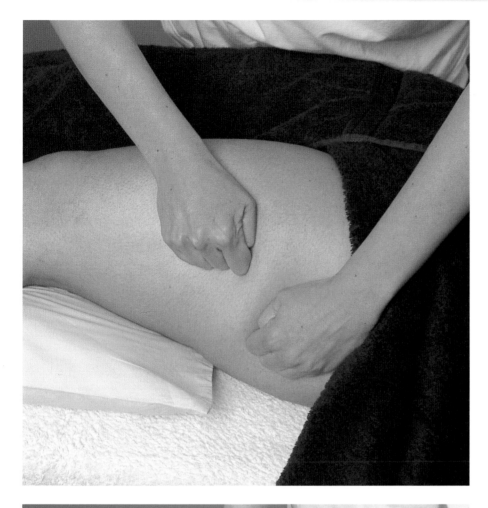

STEP 8 – knuckle the thigh
To further break down any fatty deposits and areas of cellulite, make your hands into fists and use your knuckles in a circular direction.

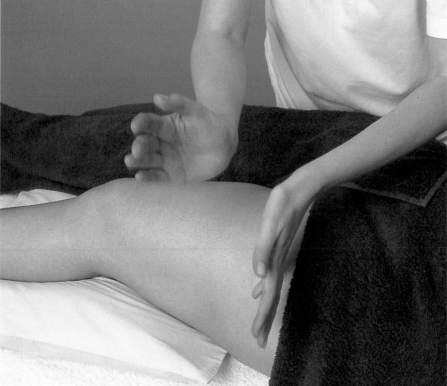

STEP 9 – tapotement on the thigh
When working on the front of the leg, percussion movements should only be carried out on the thigh avoiding the lower leg, which is bony and sensitive. Cup, hack, flick and pound the thigh to improve the circulation, reduce fatty deposits and induce muscle tone.

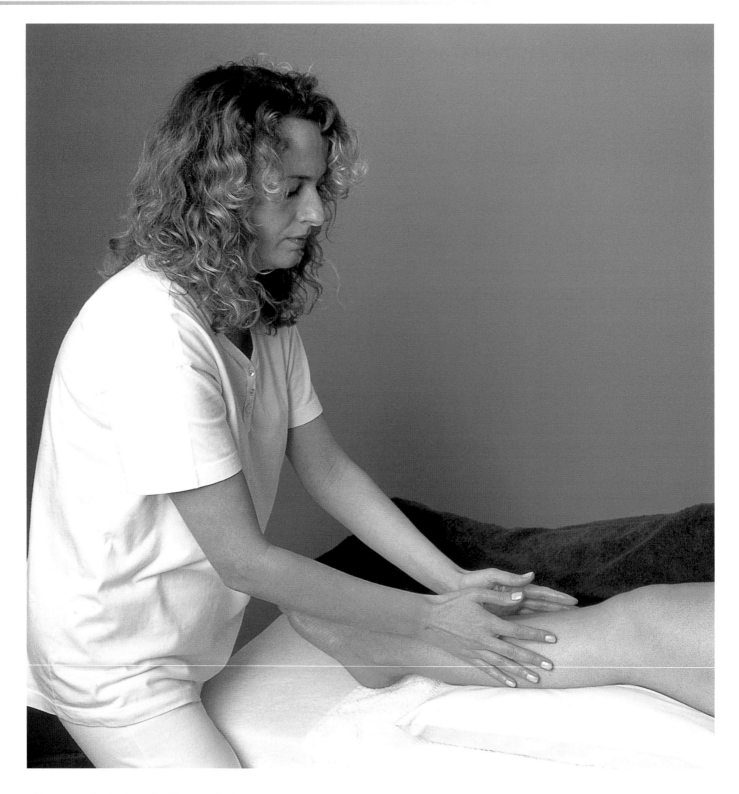

STEP 10 – the final touch effleurage the leg
Stroke the entire leg from the ankle to the top of the thigh to ensure that any remaining
toxins are thoroughly dispersed. Gradually decrease your pressure with each stroke so that
your fingertips are barely touching the skin. Allow your hands to come to rest on the foot
and gently squeeze it before lifting your hands slowly and gently away. Repeat the entire
sequence on the other leg.

MASSAGE OF THE ABDOMEN

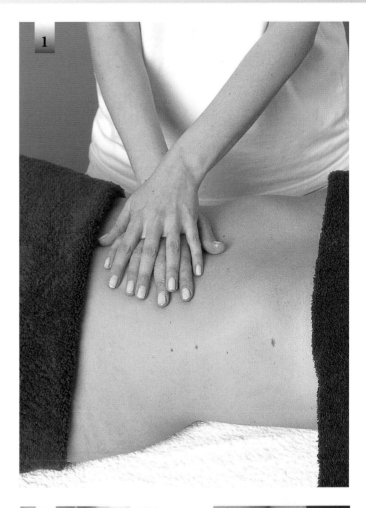

BENEFITS OF ABDOMINAL MASSAGE

● Digestive problems such as constipation, irritable bowel syndrome and flatulence can improve.

● Massage helps to restore muscle tone so that the abdomen flattens and the internal organs can be held in a normal position.

● Stretch marks and scar contratures can be prevented or reduced to a minimum.

● Fluid retention, such as experienced with pre-menstrual syndrome, may be relieved.

● Tension is relieved and emotions, which may be stored in the abdomen, can be brought to the surface and released.

WHEN TO EXERCISE CAUTION

● During pregnancy. If there is a risk or history of miscarriage take particular care over the abdomen for the first three months. Massage is excellent during pregnancy encouraging a strong bond between parent and child and soothing mother and baby.

● Avoid recent scar tissue.

● Never massage the abdomen in the presence of inflammatory condition such as gastritis.

● If there is an infectious skin condition or any unexplained lumps never massage the abdomen.

● If the bladder is full then suggest a visit to the bathroom prior to the abdominal massage.

● Talking and laughing should be discouraged otherwise the muscles will tighten making treatment of the abdomen very difficult.

STEP 1 – tuning in
Place your hands flat down on the navel, one on top of the other, and take a few deep breaths. (1)

STEP 2 – effleurage (one hand on top of the other)
Make sure that you are positioned on the right hand side of the receiver. This enables you to work around the colon in the correct direction. With one hand on top of the other, start to circle the abdomen slowly and gently in a clockwise direction. Gradually increase the size of your circular movements so that you encompass the whole of the abdomen. As the receiver relaxes you may increase the depth and intensity of your effleurage.(2)

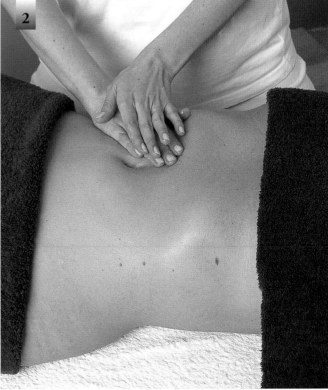

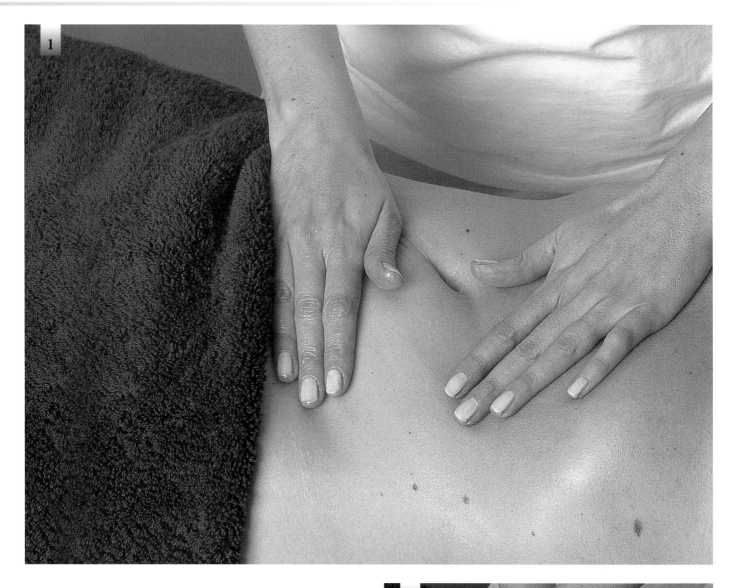

STEP 3 – effleurage (one hand following behind the other)
Now stroke the abdomen in a circular direction with one hand
following the other still in a clockwise direction. Commence with
your right hand. (1)

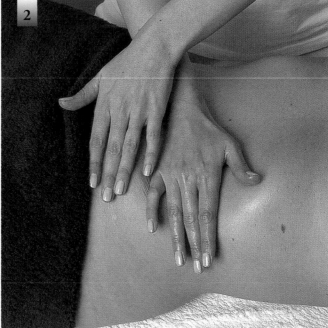

As you stroke round in a circle, your arms will cross over and you
will need to lift one hand gently over your other hand. (2)

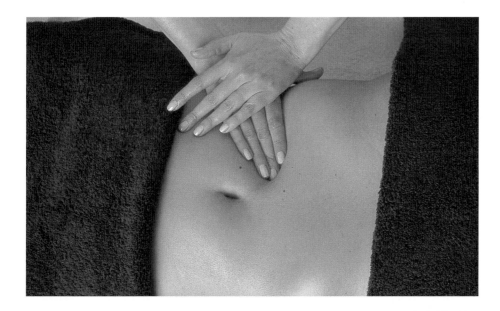

STEP 4 –colon massage
Gentle circular friction movements are particularly effective for relieving constipation. Place your right hand at the bottom right side of the abdomen. Put your other hand on top of your other to create stability. Using the flat surface of your three middle fingers make small circular friction movements following the colon.

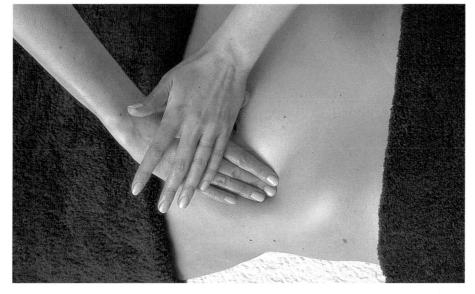

Work up the right hand side of the abdomen (ascending colon), then across the abdomen above the navel (transverse colon).

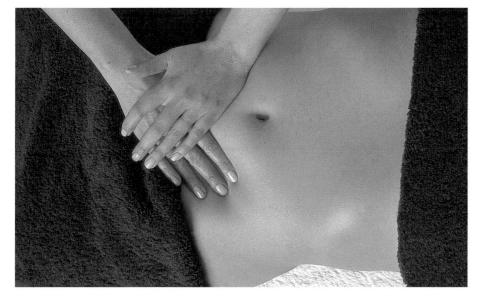

Then work down the left hand side of the abdomen (descending colon, then across the abdomen above the navel (transerve colon)

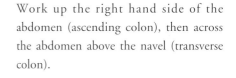

STEP 5 – drain the abdomen
This technique is excellent for bloatedness or fluid retention, which may be particularly troublesome prior to a period.

Using one hand, reach across to the far side of the abdomen and gently and slowly pull up the side of the abdomen. Then pull down diagonally across the abdomen towards the bladder. As one hand lifts off, repeat the movement with your other hand. This movement is very soothing and feels good on the back as well as the abdomen.

Repeat on the other side of the abdomen. Alternatively, you can drain both sides of the abdomen together – as shown here.

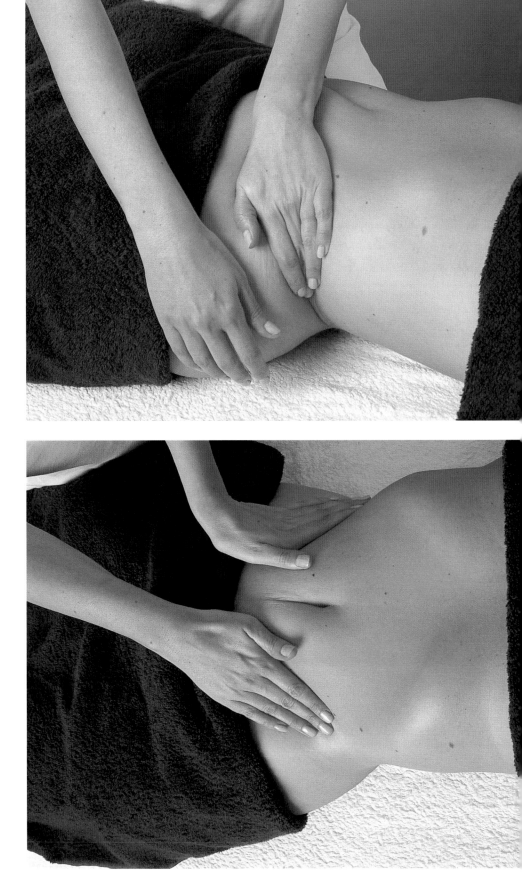

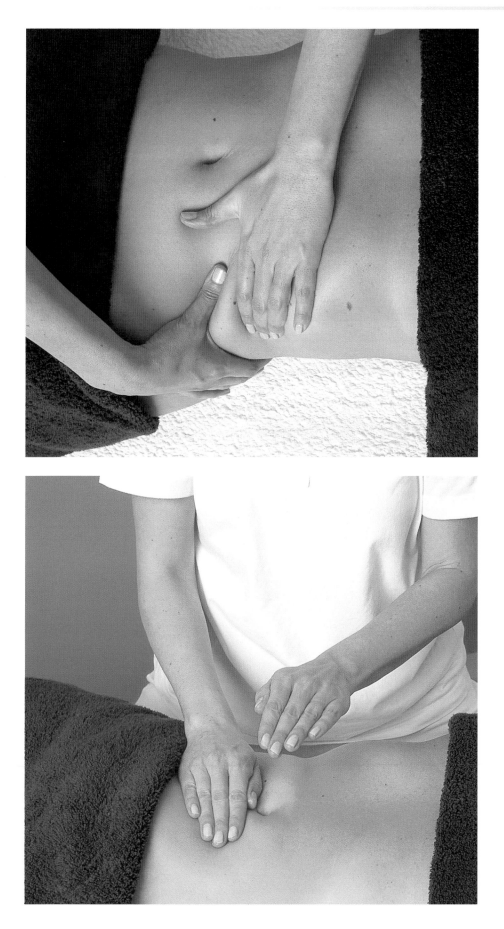

STEP 6 – knead the abdomen
Gently knead the waist and hip area, alternately squeezing and relaxing the flesh to eliminate toxins and break down fatty deposits.

STEP 7 – Cup the abdomen to increase muscle tone and to stimulate the colon. Obviously percussion movements should be VERY gentle, as the abdomen is such a delicate area. Cupping should be omitted in pregnancy and where there is inflammation or irritation in the abdomen. Gentle hacking or flicking can also be done if required.

STEP 8 – fingertip stroking
Repeat your effleurage, one hand followed by the other, using the fingertips instead of the whole of your hand. Allow your movements to become lighter and lighter until you are barely touching the skin.

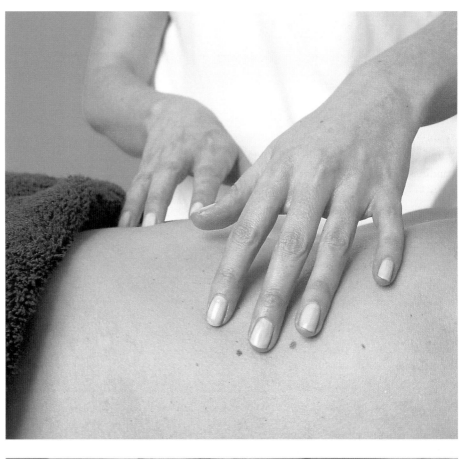

STEP 9 – the final touch
Allow your hands to come to rest on the navel, one hand on top of the other, and feel the warmth gathering. Leave them there as you notice the receiver's breathing slow down and deepen. Gently lift them away from the abdomen taking all the tension out of the body.

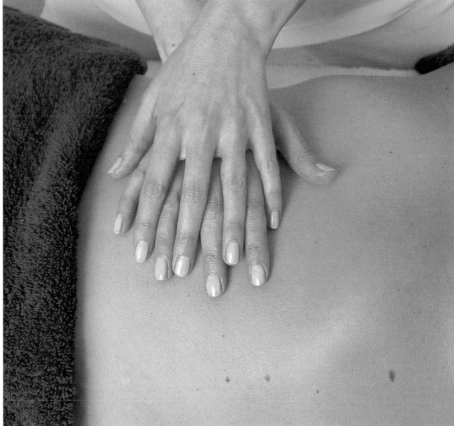

MASSAGE OF THE ARM AND HAND

BENEFITS OF ARM AND HAND MASSAGE
- Improves the circulation
- Increases the mobility of the joints and is therefore useful for conditions such as arthritis, rheumatism or old sporting injuries.
- Reduces puffiness and swelling in the arm.
- Helps to remove waste products from the tissues.
- Improves the tone of the muscles.
- Gives a general treatment to the entire body. According to hand reflexology every part of the body is reflected in miniature on the hands.
- Relieves tension and helps to release pent-up emotions.
- Helps tennis elbow, golfer's elbow, sprains, strains and overuse injuries.

WHEN TO EXERCISE CAUTION
- Never massage swollen or inflamed joints – work above and below the area.
- Avoid recent scar tissue. Old scar tissue should be treated.
- Take care over the delicate area at the front of the elbow.
- Always investigate lumps and lumps.
- Beware of infectious skin conditions.

STEP 1 – tuning in
Place both hands gently on the arm. As you breathe feel the tension melting away in the arm and hand. (1)

STEP 2 – effleurage the arm
Cup your hands across the receiver's wrist and stroke firmly up the arm from wrist to shoulder. (2)

As you reach the top of the arm open out your hands and allow them to glide lightly back down the arm. (3)

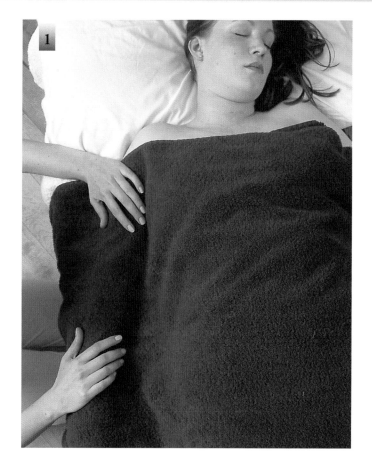

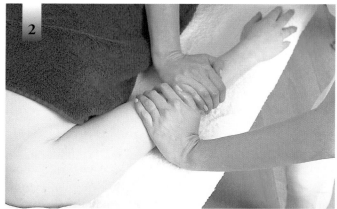

Alternatively you may effleurage the arm with one hand. Support the forearm carefully underneath with one hand as you effleurage with your other hand. Allow it to glide back down and then work with your other hand. This technique enables you to massage both sides of the arm with ease.

STEP 3 – friction the shoulder
Use both thumbs to perform slow circular friction movements all around the shoulder to increase the mobility of the joint and break down old scar tissue.

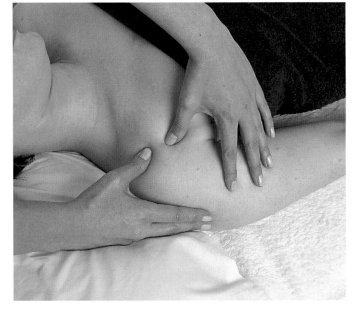

STEP 4 – petrissage the upper arm
Work with both hands to rhythmically squeeze and bring the muscle towards you to cleanse any waste products that have accumulated in the tissues.

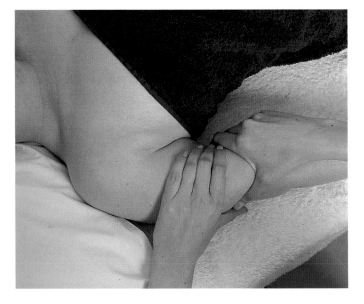

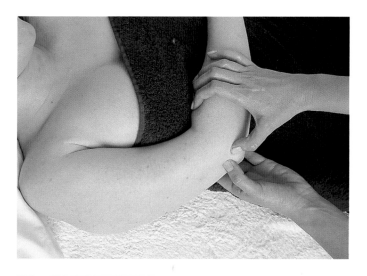

STEP 5 – loosen the elbow

To work on the elbow bend the receiver's arm and place the forearm across the body so that it is supported on the receiver's upper abdomen. Make circular friction movements all around the elbow joint to loosen it and relieve pain. Remember that if the elbow is painful then only work above and below it.

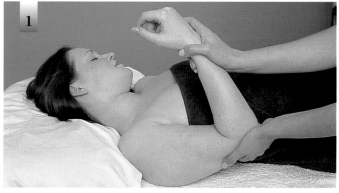

STEP 6 – move the elbow

Support the arm with one hand and with your other hand gently take it slowly into flexion (1) and extension. (2)

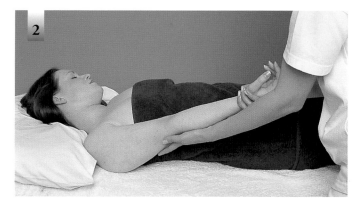

STEP 7 – effleurage the forearms

Leaving the receiver's upper arm down, elevate the forearm and support it with one hand. Use your other hand to stroke firmly from the wrist to the elbow.

If there is enough flesh then you may also gently knead the forearm from the wrist to the elbow.

STEP 8 – friction the wrist
Use your thumbs to perform circular pressures all around the
wrist joint to loosen it.

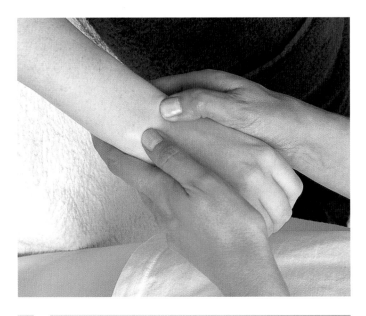

STEP 9 – mobilise the wrist
Interlock your fingers with the receiver and slowly bend the wrist
backwards and forwards, side to side (1) and then carefully circle
it in both directions.(2)

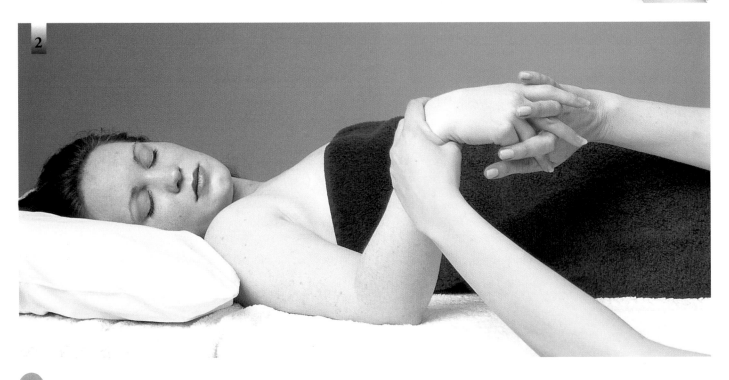

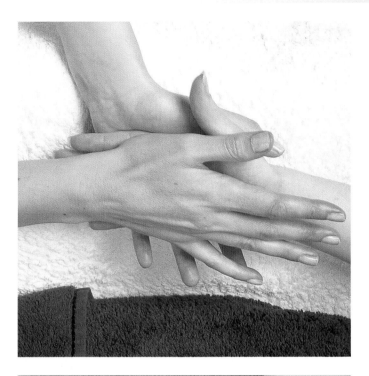

STEP 10 – effleurage the hand
Support the wrist with one hand and with your other one effleurage the top of the hand several times.

Turn the hand over and effleurage the palm of the hand. For a deeper movement on the palm you may use the heel of your hand.

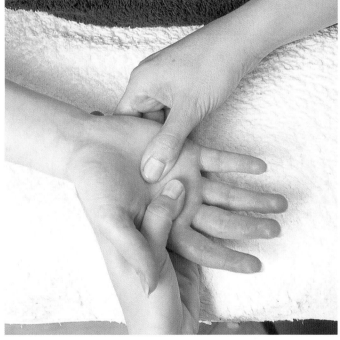

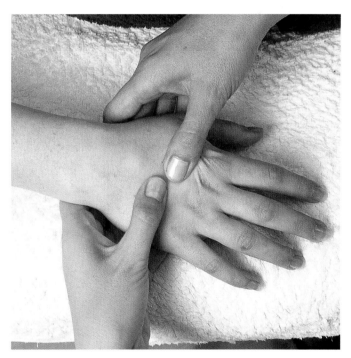

STEP 11 – stretch and open the hand
Take the receiver's hand palm uppermost in both of yours. Commence at the wrist with your thumbs flat on the palm, fingers underneath. Slide your thumbs out to the side gently opening up the palm of the hand. Repeat this movement in rows until you reach the base of the fingers.

Now turn the hand over and repeat these movements on the top of the hand. These movements are excellent for those who use their hands constantly in their day-to-day activities – e.g. typing or writing – or for those who play sports such as badminton or tennis where the hands are squashed around a racket. Musicians will also greatly benefit.

STEP 12 – knuckle the palm of the hand
Make a fist and with one hand and support the receiver's hand, palm uppermost, with your other hand. Using your knuckles, work into the palm with circular movements. This technique loosens up the muscles, joints and tendons as well as increasing the flexibility of the hand.

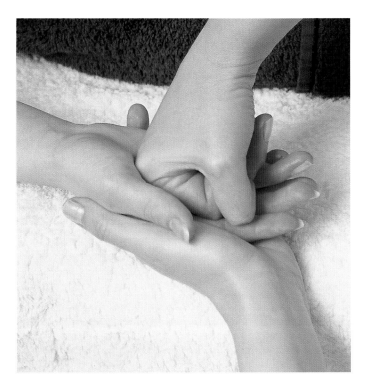

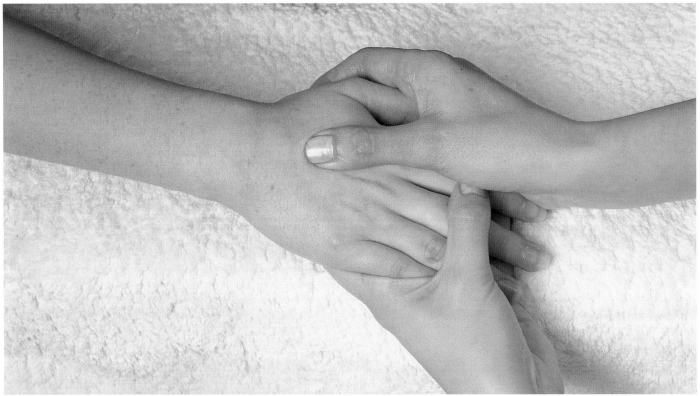

STEP 13 – stroke between the tendons
Turn the hand over and support it with one hand. You are going to start at the base of the fingers and work down towards the wrist. Use the thumb or index finger of your free hand to work along each of the furrows between the tendons.

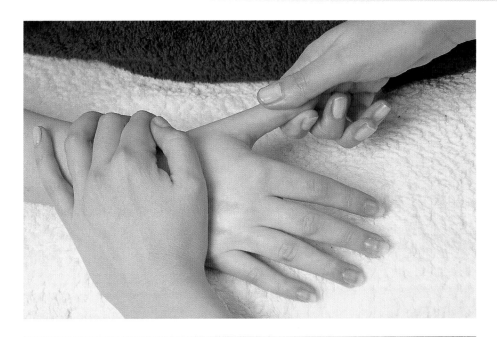

STEP 14 – stretch the fingers
Hold the receiver's hand palm down with one hand. Gently and slowly stretch and squeeze each finger individually, working from the knuckle to the tip.

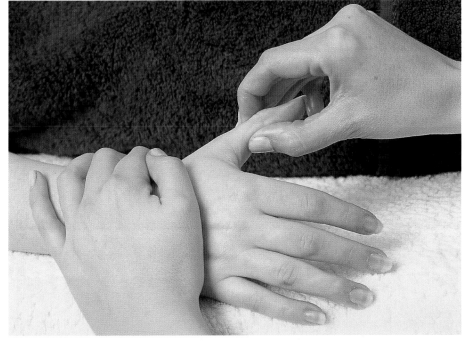

STEP 15 – friction the fingers and thumb
Using your thumb and index finger, perform gentle circular movements around each finger joint.

STEP 16 – mobilise the finger and thumb joints
Very gently flex and extend each finger and thumb joint. There are two joints in the thumb and three in each finger.

STEP 17 – circling
Circle the fingers and thumb individually both clockwise and anti-clockwise.

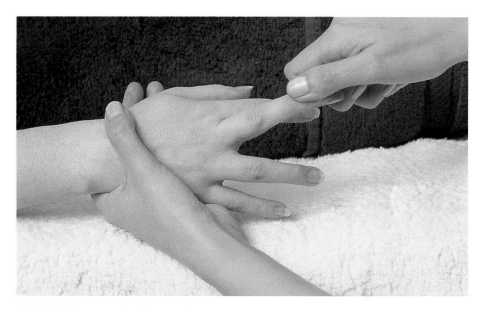

STEP 18 – effleurage
Stroke firmly up the arm from the fingers to the shoulder. Glide back with a feather light touch. Repeat your movements with decreasing pressure until there is virtually no pressure at all.

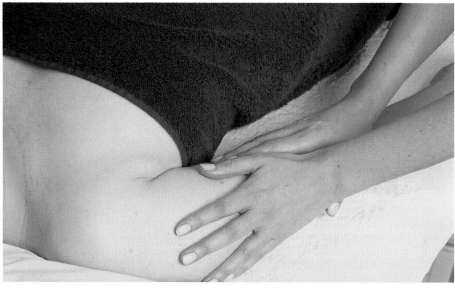

STEP 19 – the final touch – fingertips stroking
Fingertips stroke slowly down the arm and hand using just your fingertips. To end your arm and hand massage, sandwich the receiver's hand between your palms and squeeze gently.

Repeat on the other arm and hand.

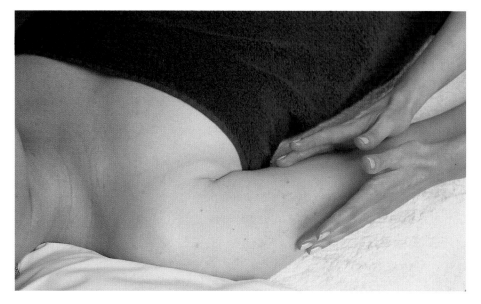

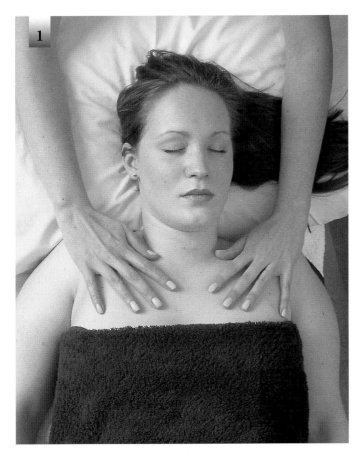

MASSAGE OF THE UPPER CHEST AND NECK

BENEFITS OF CHEST AND NECK MASSAGE

● Opens up the chest, reducing excessive tightness and allowing the breathing to slow down and deepen. Conditions such as asthma, panic attacks and hyperventilation can be improved.

● Encourages the elimination of toxins and mucus – excellent for coughs and colds.

● Releases pent-up emotions, which are often stored in the chest area.

● Improves the mobility of the neck.

● Neck massage relieves and reduces the frequency of headaches.

● Induces muscular tone.

● Improves the circulation to the head.

WHEN TO EXERCISE CAUTION

● Avoid swollen or inflamed areas.

● Never massage contagious skin conditions.

● Do not press directly on an infected area such as a boil.

● A medically qualified doctor should always examine lumps and bumps.

● Avoid recent scars.

● Take care over delicate areas – both the chest and neck are often very sensitive.

STEP 1 – tuning in
Lower your hands gently down onto the receiver's shoulders and take a few deep breaths. (1)

STEP 2 – open up the chest
Commence in the centre of the chest, both palms facing downwards. (2)

Stroke from the centre of the chest outward towards the armpits. Allow your hands to glide back with no pressure.

STEP 3 – knuckle the chest
Curl your hands into loose fists and work all over the chest area, making GENTLE circular movements to loosen up the chest muscles.

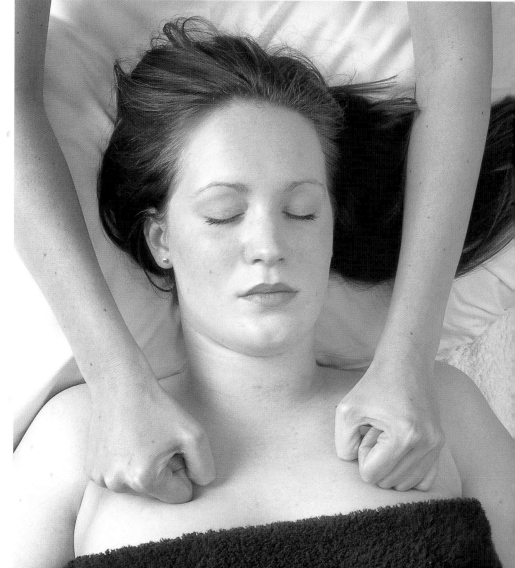

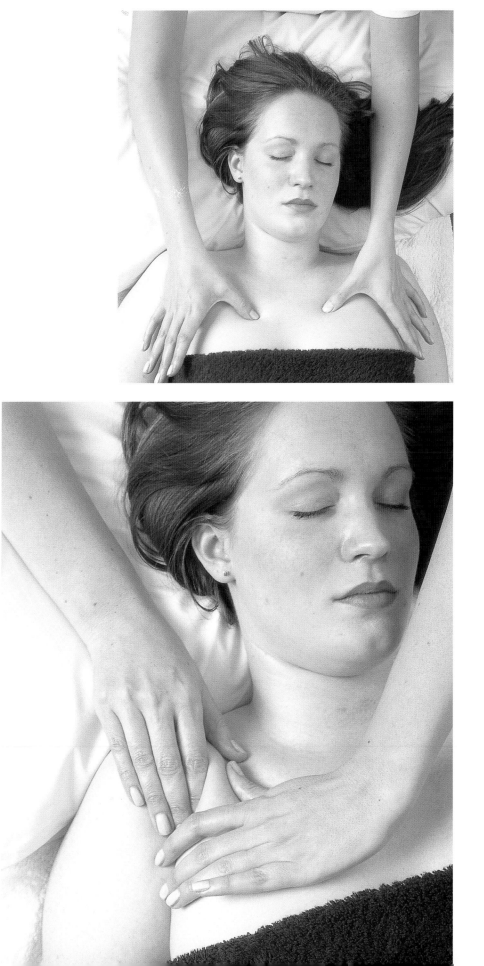

STEP 4 – friction under the clavicles (collar bones)
Place the pads of both thumbs in the centre of the chest below the clavicles. Perform gentle circular friction movements working out towards the shoulders.

STEP 5 – knead the chest
Using alternate hands, gently knead the fleshy area in front of the armpit. Slide your hands over to repeat on the opposite side. This will release further tension from the chest.

STEP 6 – stretch the shoulders
Place your hands on top of the shoulders and push them down GENTLY towards the massage surface. Now cup your hands around the shoulders and push them down GENTLY towards the feet. These movements are marvellous for hunched-up shoulders.

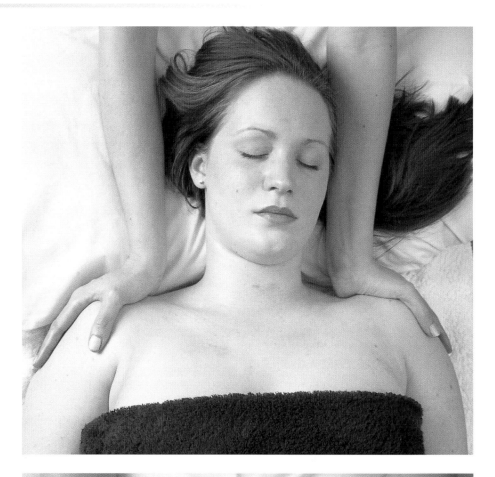

STEP 7 – loosen the neck
Place one hand either side of the receiver's neck and reach under it so that your fingertips are touching. Using both hands, gently pull up the sides of the neck towards you. Feel the tension dissolving away.

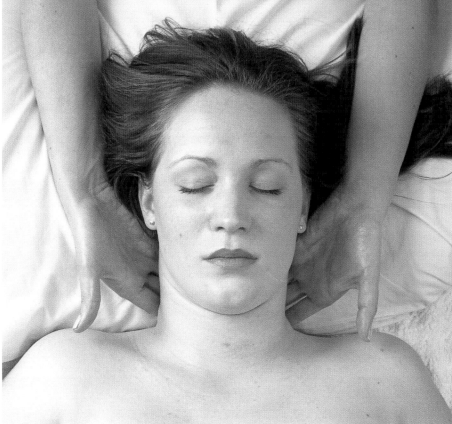

STEP 8 – side stroke the neck
Turn the head to one side and place both hands at the base of the skull. Stroke one hand down the side of the neck and as it reaches the shoulder, stroke down with your other hand.

Repeat on the other side of the neck.

STEP 9 – stretch the neck
When stretching the neck, always do it gradually and gently. Never jerk or suddenly pull the neck. Cup both hands under the head with your fingers pointing downward and pull the head slowly towards you as you lean backwards. Gradually release the stretch.

STEP 10 – the final touch – stroking
Using just your fingertips, stroke gently down the neck and out across the chest.

FACE MASSAGE

BENEFITS OF FACE MASSAGE

- Soothes away anxiety and tension.
- Relieves headaches.
- Unblocks the sinuses and alleviates nasal congestion.
- Tones up the muscles – the rejuvenating effects of a face massage provides an alternative to a facelift.
- Improves the circulation to the skin – the complexion takes on a healthy glow.
- Circulation to the head and brain is stimulated, aiding concentration and memory.
- Cleanses waste deposits from the face.
- Reduces puffiness, particularly around the eye area.

WHEN TO EXERCISE CAUTION

- Use only light pressure on the delicate areas of the face – especially where the skin is thin or over broken veins.
- Never massage over contact lenses.
- Avoid areas of infection such as spots or boils.
- Check out any unusual moles or lumps.
- Do not massage over recent scars.
- Avoid areas of inflammation.

STEP 1 – tuning in
Rest cupped hands on the receiver's forehead, almost without touching, and breathe deeply. (1)

STEP 2 – effleurage the forehead
Bring the palms of your hands together, fingers interlocking, and place them on the receiver's forehead. Gently draw them apart, stroking outwards across the forehead towards the temples. Allow your hands to glide back with no pressure.(2)

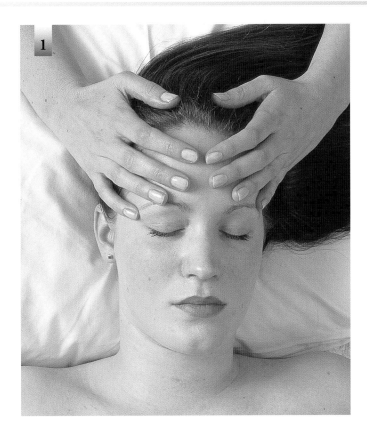

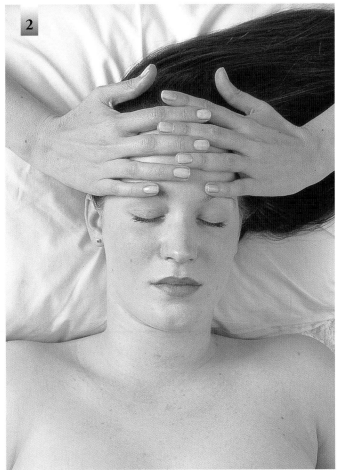

STEP 3 – effleurage the cheeks
Place one hand on each cheek, and with your fingertips and palms stroke outwards across the cheeks.

STEP 4 – effleurage the chin
Place the hands in the centre of the chin palms down, fingertips facing each other. Stroke outwards across the chin, moulding your hands to the contours of the face.

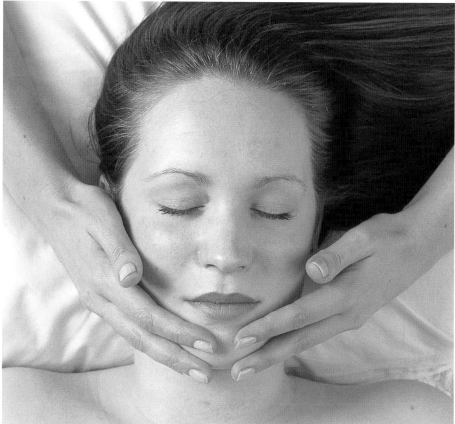

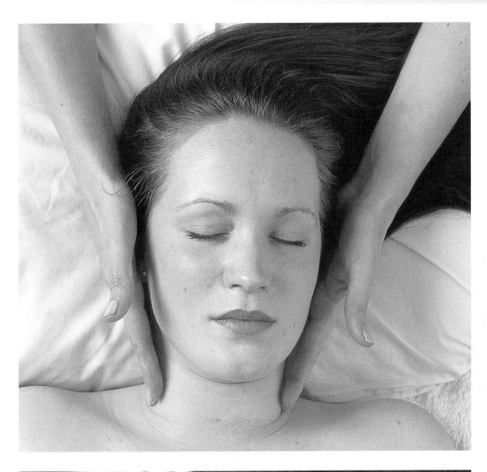

Continue stroking down the neck towards the shoulders.

The previous movements are highly effective for removing tension from the face. If you find it awkward using your palms and fingertips then you can use the relaxed fingertips of the back of your hands.

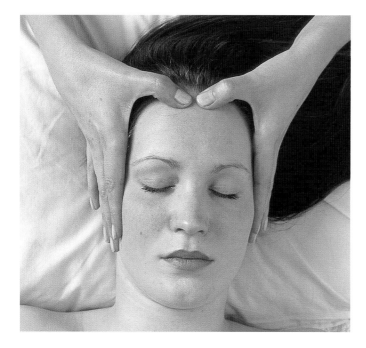

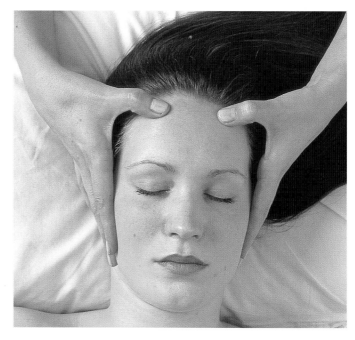

STEP 5 – drain the face
Place the pads of your thumbs on the centre of the forehead just below the hairline.

Working outwards in a row, press and release at intervals of approximately one inch.

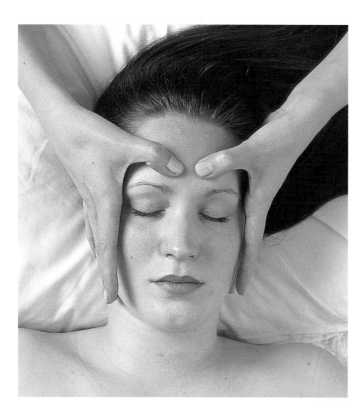

After your first row, bring the thumbs back to the centre of the forehead but place them slightly lower down. Repeat your pressing and releasing in rows until you reach the eyebrows.

Now effleurage the forehead gently to eliminate any accumulated waste products that you have released.

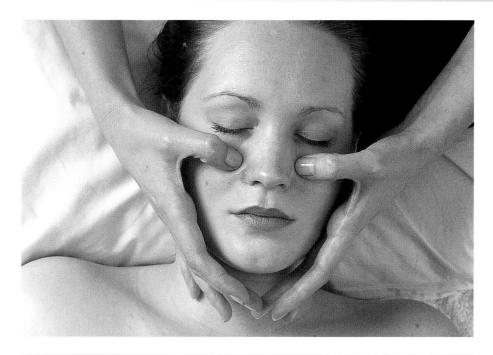

CHEEKS

Repeat the previous technique, this time covering the cheek area. Commence just under the eyes working outwards across the cheeks towards the ears.

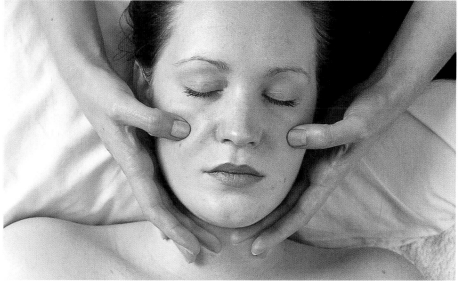

Work in horizontal strips to cover the entire area. Then effleurage the cheeks gently to drain away the toxins.

CHIN AND JAW

Repeat the previous technique, commencing under the mouth in the centre of the chin. Press and release working outwards in horizontal rows. Then effleurage the waste products away.

STEP 6 – unblock the nasal passages
Using both thumbs, stroke gently down the sides of the nose. This is excellent for clearing away congestion.

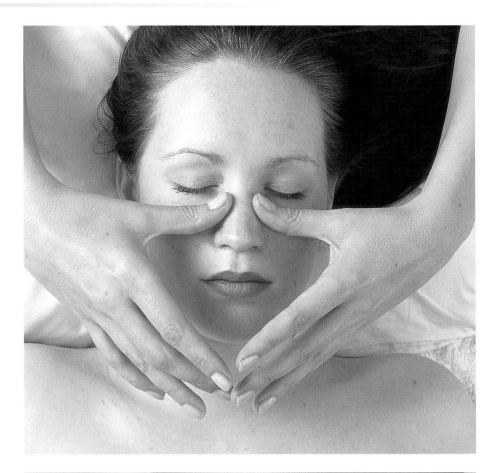

STEP 7 – squeeze the jaw
Commencing in the centre of the jaw, gently squeeze it between your thumbs and index fingers to tone up the jaw line.

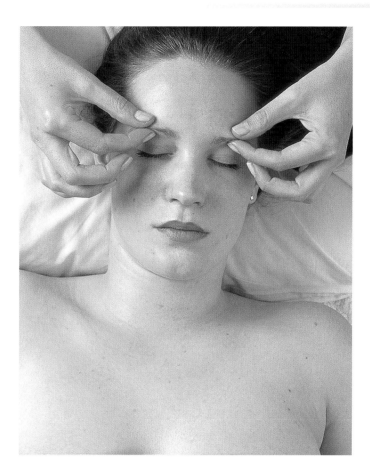

STEP 8 – squeeze the eyebrows
Commencing at the inside of the eyebrows, gently squeeze the
brow bone working outwards until you reach the outer edges.

STEP 9 – circle the eyes
With your fingertips, make very gentle circular movements
around the eyes with virtually no pressure.

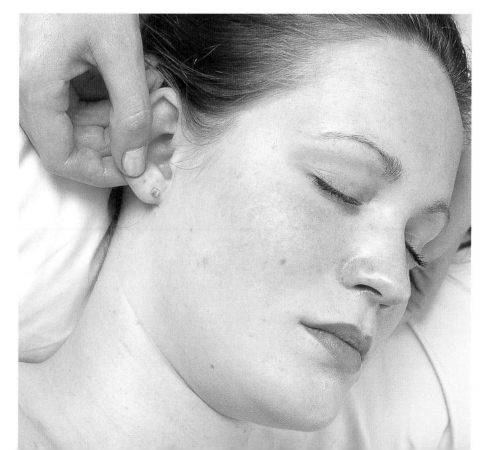

STEP 10 – massage the ears
Using your thumbs and forefingers,
massage all over the ears. Then stretch
and release them gently.

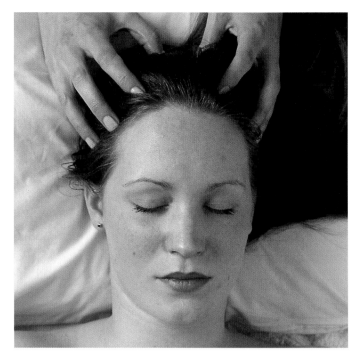

STEP 11 – circle the mouth
Make very gentle circular movements with your fingertips all around the mouth to release tension and to reduce fine lines.

STEP 12 –release tension in the scalp
Using the pads of the fingertips, massage the scalp with deep circular friction movements slowly and firmly from the top of the forehead around to the base of the skull. This helps to relieve headaches, release tension and also stimulates hair growth.

STEP 13 – pull the hair
Stroke the hair with your fingertips and then gently clasp small sections of the hair near to the roots and pull them slowly towards you. Pulling the hair helps to release the last remaining tension.

STEP 14 – the final touch
Place your hands on the temples and rest them there with barely any pressure. Lift them away from the head very slowly.

EASY REFERENCE GUIDE

BACK OF THE BODY

BACK OF THE LEGS

1 tune in
2 effleurage the leg
3 effleurage the calf
4 friction the calf
5 pick up and squeeze the calf
6 pick up and roll the calf
7 wring the calf
8 effleurage the leg
9 effleurage the thigh
10 knead the thigh
11 knuckle the thigh
12 pound the thigh
13 cup the leg
14 hack the leg
15 the final touch - fingertip effleurage

Repeat on the other leg.

THE BACK

1 tune in
2 effleurage the whole back
3 circular effleurage on both sides
of the back
4 friction on the spinal muscles
5 heel of hand stroking down both sides
of the back
6 effleurage lower back and buttocks
7 friction the top of the pelvis
8 petrissage the buttocks and waist
9 cup, hack and pound the buttocks
and waist
10 effleurage the shoulders
11 friction around the shoulder blade
12 petrissage the shoulders
13 pick up the neck
14 effleurage the whole back
15 the final touch - fingertip stroking

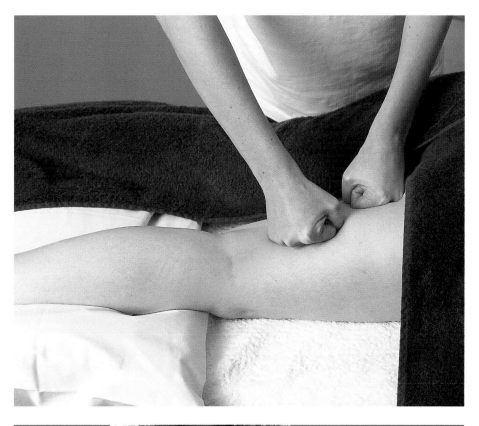

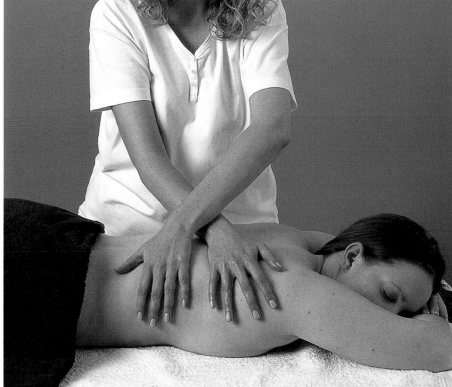

FRONT OF THE BODY

FEET

1 tune in

2 effleurage the foot

3 metatarsal kneading

4 spread the foot

5 stroke the inside of the foot

6 toes

7 ankle loosening

8 ankle rotation

9 foot vibrations

10 the final touch - effleurage

Repeat on the other foot.

FRONT OF THE LEGS

1 tune in

2 effleurage the leg

3 effleurage the lower leg

4 thumb circling the knee cap

5 friction the knee cap

6 effleurage the thigh

7 petrissage the thigh

8 knuckle the thigh

9 tapotement on the thigh

10 the final touch - effleurage

Repeat on the other leg.

ABDOMEN

1 tune in

2 circular effleurage - one hand on top of the other

3 circular effleurage - one hand following the other

4 colon massage

5 drain the abdomen

6 knead the abdomen

7 gentle cupping and hacking

8 fingertip stroking

9 the final touch - hands rest on the navel

ARM AND HAND

1 tune in

2 effleurage the arm

3 friction the shoulder

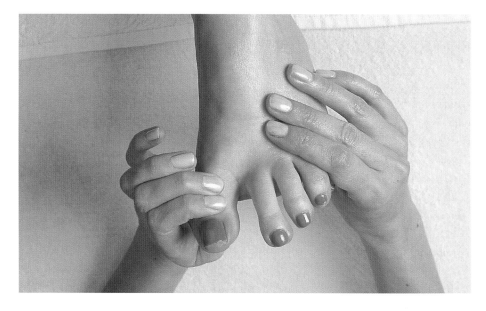

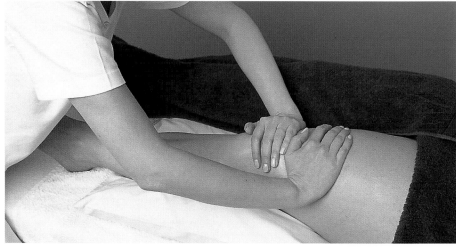

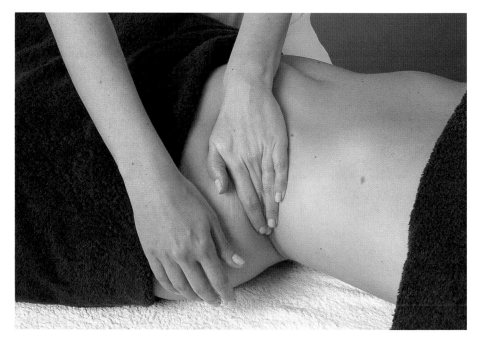

4 petrissage the upper arm
5 loosen the elbow
6 move the elbow
7 effleurage the forearm
8 friction the wrist
9 mobilise the wrist
10 effleurage the hand
11 stretch and open up the hand
12 knuckle the palm of the hand
13 stroke between the tendons
14 stretch the fingers
15 friction the fingers and thumb
16 mobilise the finger joints
17 circle the fingers and thumb
18 effleurage the hand and arm
19 the final touch - fingertip stroking

Repeat on the other arm and hand.

UPPER CHEST AND NECK
1 tune in
2 open up the chest
3 knuckle the chest
4 friction under the collar bones
5 knead the chest
6 stretch the shoulders
7 loosen the neck
8 side stroke the neck
9 stretch the neck
10 the final touch - stroking

FACE
1 tune in
2 effleurage the forehead
3 effleurage the cheeks
4 effleurage the chin
5 drain the face, cheeks, chin and jaw
6 unlock the nasal passages
7 squeeze the jaw
8 squeeze the eyebrows
9 circle the eyes
10 massage the ears
11 circle the mouth
12 release tension in the scalp
13 pull the hair
14 the final touch - rest your hands on the temples

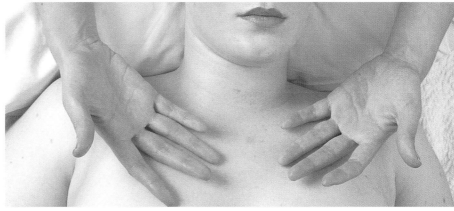

The advantage of self-massage is that you can perform it as often as you wish and whenever you want. It is an invaluable way of discovering which movements feel good, and allows you to experiment with different pressures and rhythms. The more you are able to massage your own body the better you will be at massaging others.

Unfortunately there are several disadvantages to self-massage. There is no exchange of energy from one person to another. It is also impossible to totally relax, since at least one hand will always be massaging and some areas of the body are very difficult to reach without causing discomfort.

However, if you do not have someone to massage you then it is well worth the effort to do it yourself. You may carry out the complete sequence or simply select any area that needs attention.

LEGS

Leg massage is an excellent way to relieve tired and aching muscles. It will also improve your circulation, help to prevent varicose veins and eliminate toxins. It will take you less than five minutes to massage each leg.

STEP 1. EFFLEURAGE THE WHOLE LEG
Sit down on the floor with your legs outstretched in front of you. Effleurage the leg upwards from your ankle to your thigh, moulding your hands to the contours of the leg. If you are not very supple then bend the leg slightly. (1)

STEP 2. EFFLEURAGE THE CALF MUSCLES
Still sitting on the floor, bend one leg up so that the foot is flat on the ground. Using one or both hands, effleurage from the heel to the back of your knee. (2)

STEP 3. PETRISSAGE THE CALF MUSCLES
Keep your knee bent and petrissage the calf, alternately squeezing and releasing the calf muscles. This will bring the deeper toxins to

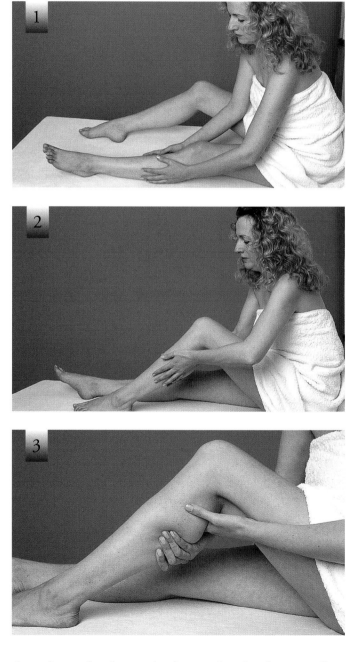

the surface so that they can be eliminated, and is also an excellent way of preventing and alleviating cramp. (3)

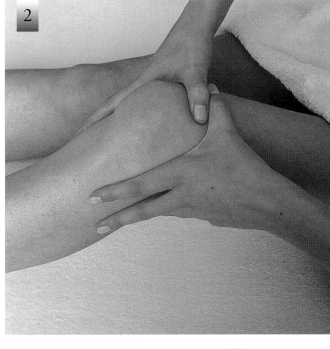

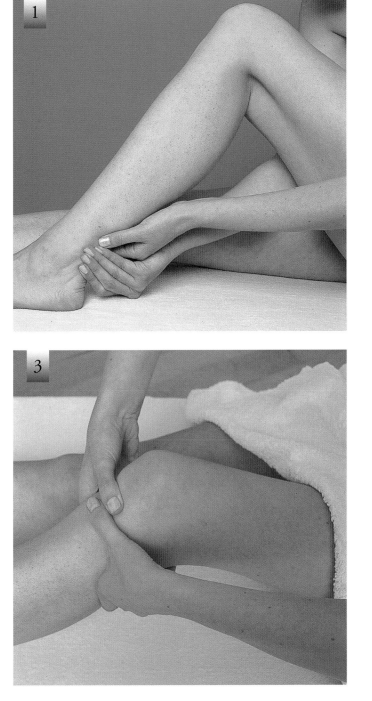

STEP 4. FRICTION THE ACHILLES TENDON
Using your fingers and thumbs, work all around the
Achilles tendon. (1)

STEP 5. CIRCLING THE KNEE
Place both thumbs just below the knee and glide them gently
around the knee, one thumb either side until they meet at
the top. (2)

STEP 6. Then circle the thumbs again until they meet
underneath the knee. (3)

STEP 7. LOOSEN THE KNEE
Use the pads of your thumbs or fingertips to work all around the
patella using small circular friction movements. This technique is
excellent for increasing flexibility of the knee joint. Do this every
day if you have arthritis or an old knee injury. (4)

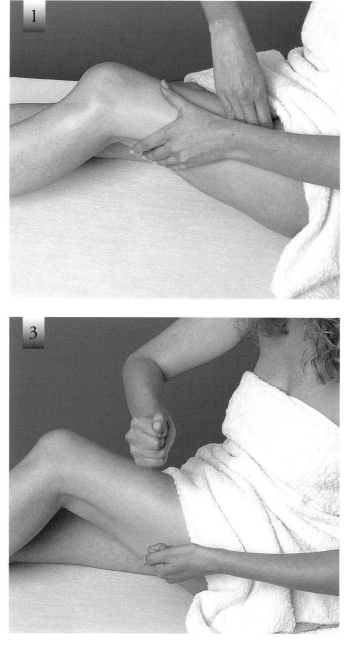

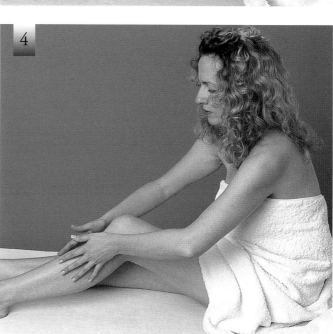

STEP 8. EFFLEURAGE THE THIGH

Firmly stroke the muscles of the thigh from the knee to the groin. Make sure that you cover all aspects – the front, the sides and the back. You may effleurage with one hand following the other or, for a firmer pressure, put one hand on top of the other. (1)

STEP 9. PETRISSAGE THE THIGH

Knead the inner, middle and outer thigh to break down fatty deposits and unsightly cellulite. Over a period of time, kneading can really improve the shape of your thighs. If there are areas of cellulite, make your hands into fists and use your knuckles in a circular direction. (2)

STEP 10. POUND THE THIGH

Clench your fists lightly and apply them to the thigh in quick succession. Pounding improves circulation as blood is brought to the surface, reduces fatty deposits and improves muscle tone. (3)

STEP 11. COMPLETION

To end the sequence, gently stroke the leg from ankle to thigh with a feather light touch. (4)

Repeat on the other leg.

THE FEET

A daily foot massage is excellent not only for de-stressing but also improves your general health since according to foot reflexology the whole of the body can be treated via the feet.

You may either sit on the floor, bed or on a chair and you need to be able to raise one foot on to the opposite knee. If you are working on the floor you may find it comfortable to place a cushion or pillow under your bent knee.

STEP 1. EFFLEURAGE THE FOOT
Place one hand on top of the foot and one under the sole. Using both hands stroke firmly up the foot working from the toes up towards the ankle and back again. (1)

STEP 2. LOOSEN THE SOLE OF THE FOOT
With your thumbs, work into the sole of the foot using small deep circular movements to loosen up the tendons and muscles. (2)

STEP 3. FRICTION THE TOES
Support the foot, with one hand and massage the joints of the toes (top and bottom) between your thumb and index finger to thoroughly loosen them. (3)

STEP 4. MOVE THE TOES
Slowly stretch each toe and then move each one individually both clockwise and anti-clockwise to increase flexibility. (4)

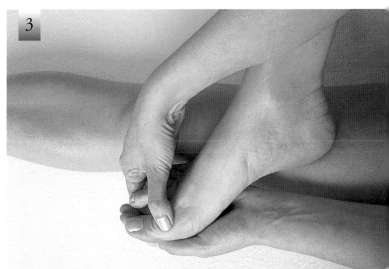

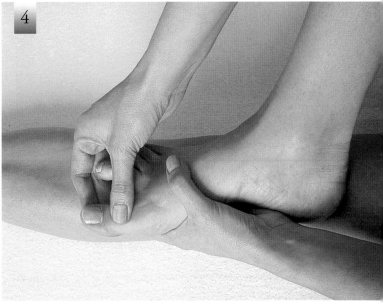

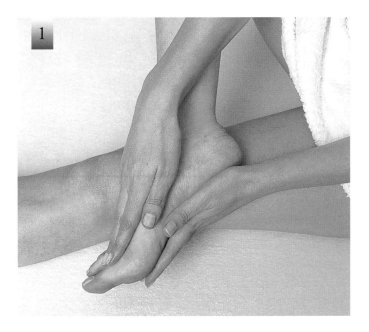

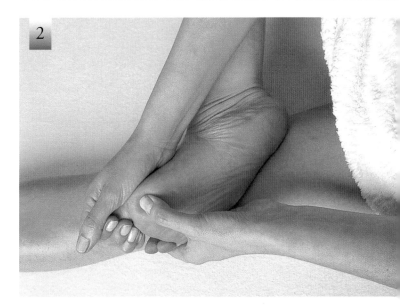

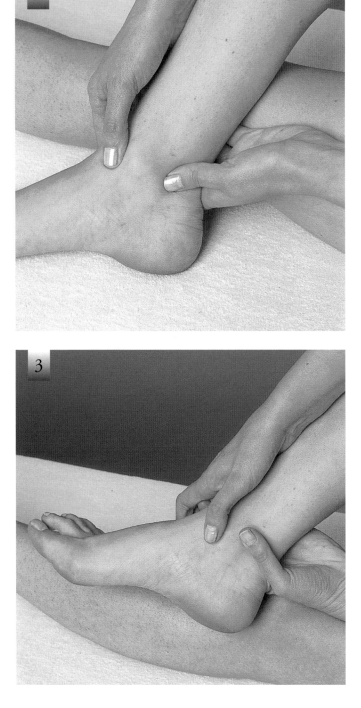

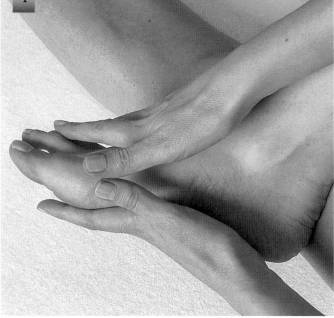

STEP 5. FRICTION THE ANKLE

Using thumbs or fingertips, massage all around the ankle joint with small deep circular movements to break down old scar tissue. (1)

STEP 6. MOVE THE ANKLE

Support the foot with one hand and slowly circle the ankle both clockwise and anti-clockwise. (2,3)

STEP 7. COMPLETION

Using just your fingertips, stroke the foot slowly from the toes to the ankle. Sandwich the foot between the palms of your hands and squeeze gently. (4)

Repeat on the other foot.

NECK AND SHOULDERS

The majority of us suffer occasionally with our neck and shoulders. Tightness in the neck can lead to restrictions and inability to move the head properly and often gives rise to headaches. This massage can be performed sitting on a bed, chair or on the floor. The neck and shoulders are easily accessible and can even be massaged through the clothes. Try working on them when watching television in the evening or travelling to work on the bus or train or whilst sitting in a traffic jam.

STEP 1. FRICTION THE BASE OF THE SKULL

Let your head relax forwards as far as is comfortable and bring your hands behind your head. Use your thumbs and fingertips to make small circular friction movements all around the base of the skull. Firm pressure in this area can get rid of headaches and prevents them from occurring. (1)

STEP 2. EFFLEURAGE THE NECK

Clasp your hands together lightly and stroke the neck outwards from the base of the skull to the shoulders. (2)

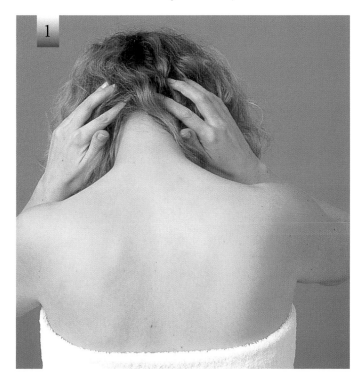

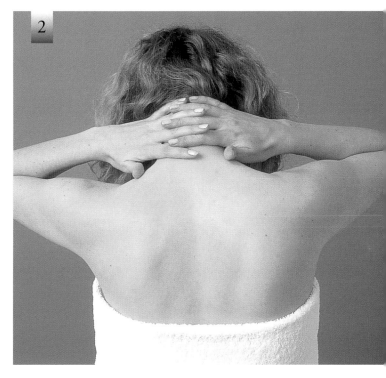

STEP 3. EFFLEURAGE THE SHOULDERS

To massage your left shoulder, place your right hand at the base of the skull and stroke down the side of the neck and over your shoulder. (3)

Then massage your right shoulder using your left hand to thoroughly relax the muscles.

1

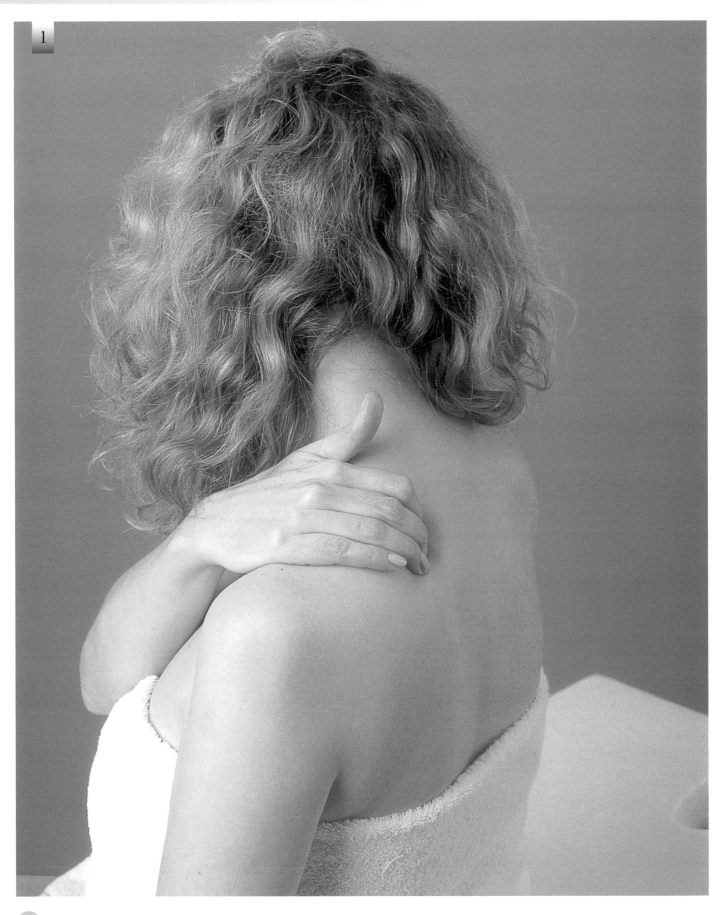

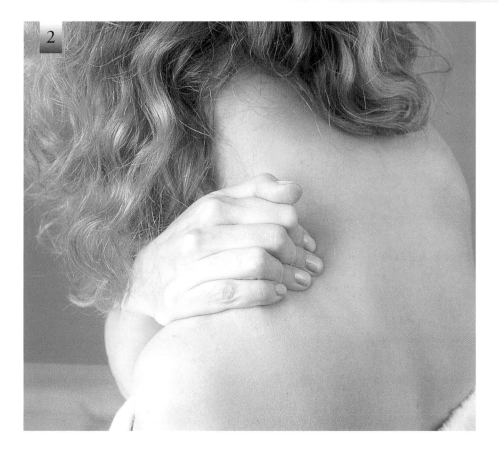

STEP 4. FRICTION THE SHOULDER BLADES

Reach across the front of your body with your right hand to locate your left shoulder blade. Use your fingertips to apply deep circular friction movements into the knots that are so common around the shoulder blade. (1)

Repeat on the other side.

STEP 5. KNEAD THE SHOULDERS

Squeeze and release the left shoulder by reaching across the front of the body with your right hand picking up as much flesh as possible. Now knead the other shoulder. (2)

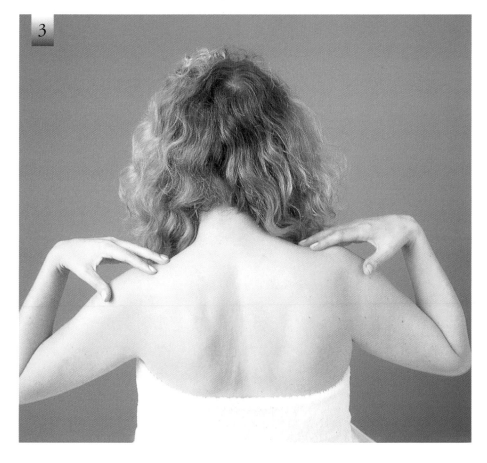

STEP 6. COMPLETION

Place one hand either side of the top of the neck and stroke both hands slowly down the neck and over the shoulders. (3)

A R M S A N D H A N D S

Massage of the arms and hands is wonderful for people who use them extensively in their work – e.g. hairdressers, gardeners, keyboard operators, writers, etc. Treatment can also prevent sports injuries from occurring.

STEP 1. EFFLEURAGE THE ARM
Rest your hand gently on your lap and effleurage the whole arm from the wrist up to the shoulder. (1)

STEP 2. KNEAD THE UPPER ARM

Pick up and squeeze as much flesh as you can on your upper arm to break down fatty deposits and improve muscle tone. (2)

STEP 3. DEEP STROKING TO THE FOREARM
With your thumb on one side of the arm and your fingers underneath, apply deep stroking movements from the wrist to the elbow. If you find any tight areas then gently loosen them by performing small deep circular friction movements on the troublesome area. (3)

STEP 4. FRICTION AND MOVE THE ELBOW
To loosen the elbow, make small circular friction movements all around the elbow with your fingertips, working deeply into any tight areas. (4)

STEP 5. MOVE THE ELBOW
Cup under the elbow with your hand and gently and slowly bend and stretch the forearm to improve flexibility. (5)

STEP 6. LOOSEN THE WRIST
Use your thumbs or fingertips to perform circular pressures all around the wrist joint to loosen it up. (6)

STEP 7. MOVE THE WRIST Now gently circle your wrist both clockwise and anti-clockwise. (7)

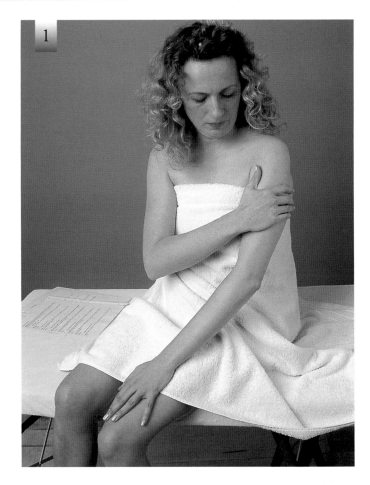

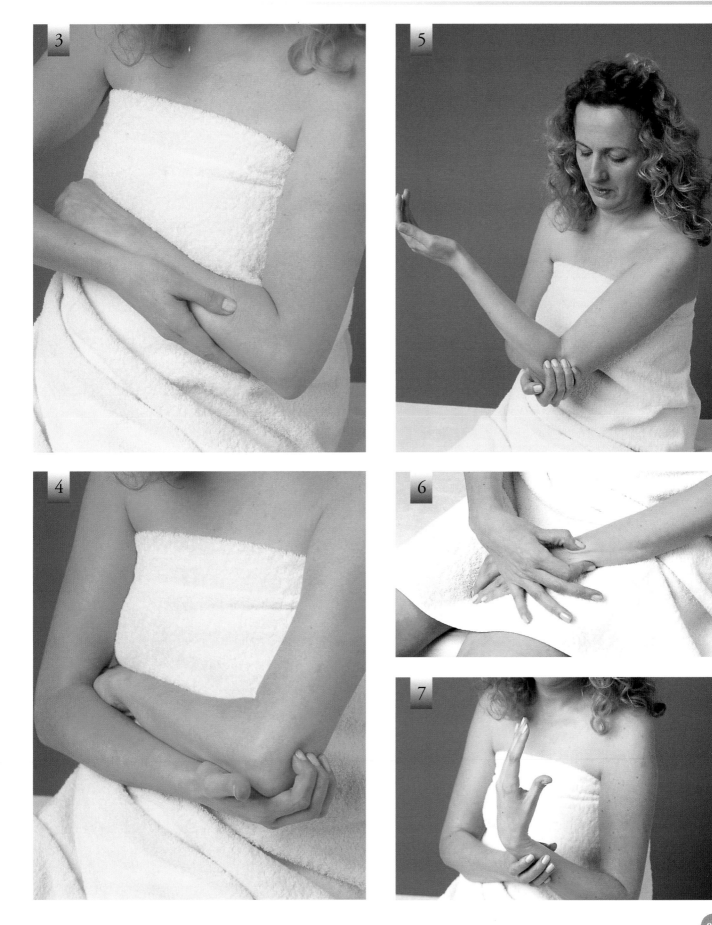

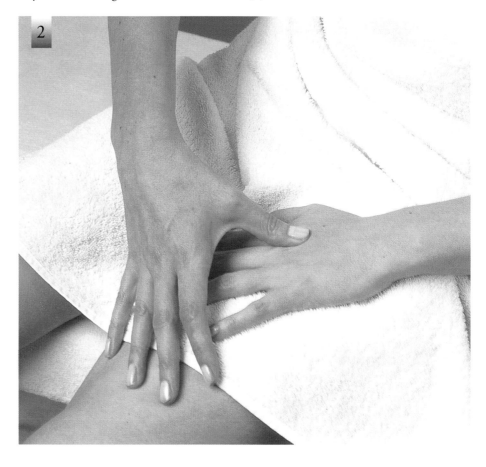

STEP 8. WORK INTO THE PALM OF THE HAND

With a loosely clenched fist, work into the palm of your hand with gentle circular movements. (1)

STEP 9. STROKING BETWEEN THE TENDONS

Turn the hand over and, using your thumb or fingertips, work along each of the furrows between the tendons from the knuckles to the wrist. (2)

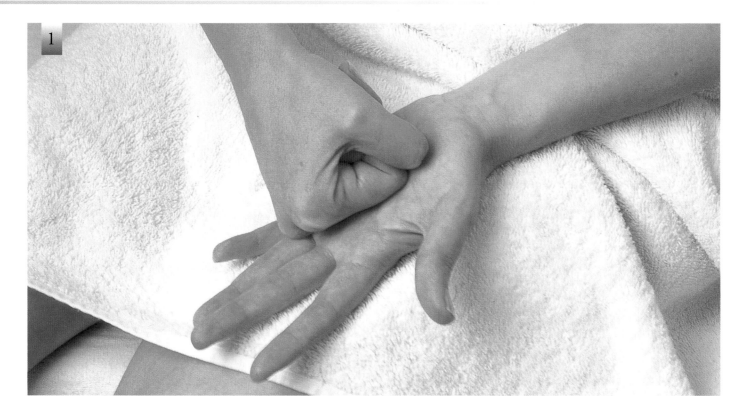

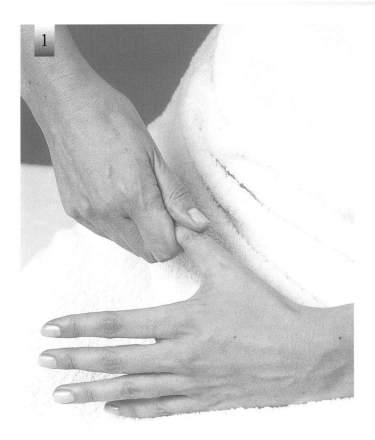

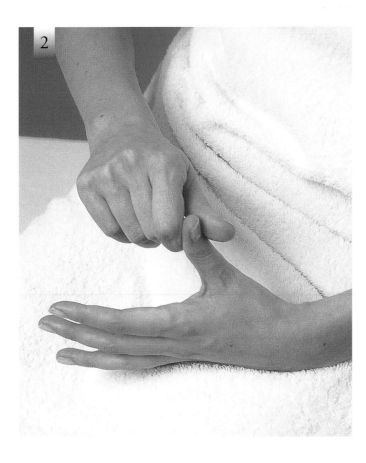

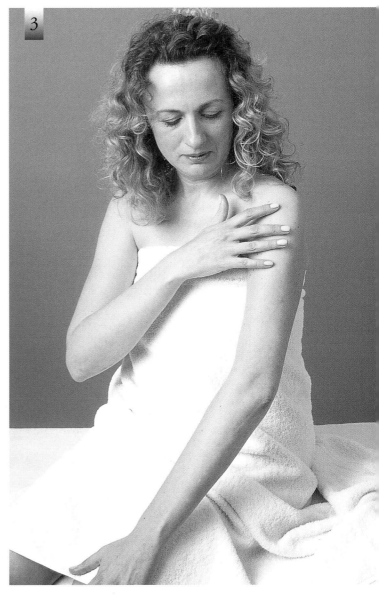

STEP 10. LOOSEN AND MOVE THE FINGERS
AND THUMB

Gently and slowly stretch each finger and thumb individually, working from the knuckle to the tip, using your thumb and index finger.(3)Then gently circle them in one direction and then in the opposite direction. (4) Using just your fingertips, gently stroke up the arm gently from fingers to the shoulder. Make sure that you cover all aspects of the arm. (5)

FACE AND SCALP

STEP 1. EFFLEURAGE
Place both hands on your forehead, fingertips facing each other and stroke out across the forehead. (1) Then stroke outwards across the cheeks. (2) Finally stroke across the chin. (3)

STEP 2. GENTLE FRICTION
Using your fingertips, perform gentle circular friction movements starting at the hairline and working all the way down the face until you reach the jaw line. (4)

STEP 3. TONE THE EYEBROWS AND CHIN
With your thumbs and index fingers, gently squeeze all along the brow bone. (5) Then repeat the squeezing along your jaw line to help prevent the development of a double chin. (6)

STEP 4. EYES
Using your index or middle fingers, start just below the corner of the eye and stroke gently outwards. This helps to reduce puffiness around the eyes and should be carried out very gently, as this is such a delicate area. (7)

STEP 5. SCALP FRICTION
Rub the scalp vigorously all over in a circular motion with your fingertips. Scalp friction helps to release toxins from the scalp and encourages the hair to grow. (8)

STEP 6. COMPLETION
Place the heel of both hands over your eyes. Hold your hands there for a few seconds allowing your eyes to completely relax. When you take your hands away you will feel remarkably revitalised. (9)

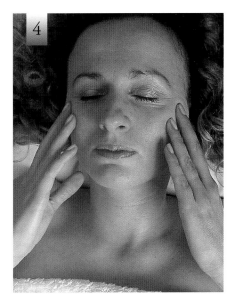

therapeutic massage
for Common Ailments

Therapeutic massage has a wide range of physiological and psychological advantages and can be used to treat a whole host of common diseases. However, where a problem is persistent or serious then a medically qualified doctor should always be consulted. This chapter outlines some of the ailments that can be successfully treated with massage. Eight essential oils were outlined in the first chapter, and ONLY these are included throughout the chapter.

CIRCULATORY PROBLEMS

HIGH BLOOD PRESSURE

High blood pressure is a fairly common disorder with a variety of causes. Stress is a major factor, which causes the muscles to contract and constrict the arteries. Dietary factors such as saturated fats and too much salt can also elevate cholesterol levels and lead to hardening of the arteries. Family history and smoking are also contributory factors.

MASSAGE TREATMENT

Massage is a well-accepted therapy for reducing high blood pressure – regular treatment encourages it to reduce – sometimes quite dramatically. When we are anxious or emotional this causes the blood pressure to rise and the deep relaxation afforded by massage will calm even the tensest individuals.

● A full body massage at least once a week should be given. Brisk stimulating movements such as cupping and hacking should be omitted from the sequence.

● A great deal of gentle effleurage should be used particularly over the back during the treatment to calm, soothe and relax the receiver. (1)

● It is highly beneficial to massage either the feet or the hands daily to ensure a calm state of mind. (2)

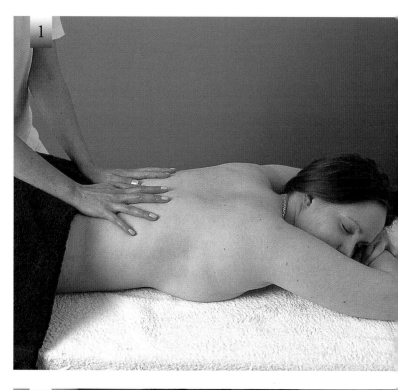

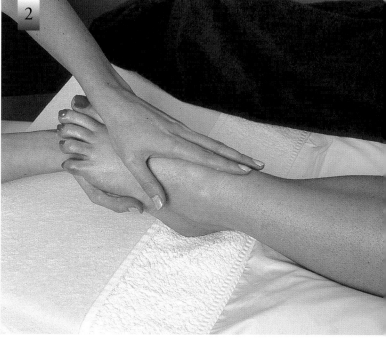

Essential oils of chamomile, geranium or lavender can be added to the massage oil to enhance the relaxation effects either singly or blended together.

To 10 mls (two teaspoons) of carrier oil add:
1 drop chamomile
1 drop geranium
1 drop lavender

OTHER ADVICE
● Eat lots of fruit, vegetables, fibre (especially oats) and garlic. Avoid salt, sugar and saturated fats.
● Try to reduce stress.
● Give up smoking and reduce alcohol and caffeine.
● Take up gentle exercise such as Tai Chi and yoga.

VARICOSE VEINS
Varicose veins occur when the valves in the veins are faulty and are unable to keep the blood from flowing backwards. They affect four times as many women as men with nearly 50% of middle-aged adults affected. Pregnancy, long periods of standing, obesity, genetic weakness and constipation and are all causes of varicose veins.

MASSAGE TREATMENT
You must never carry out the more vigorous movements such as cupping or hacking. Never press directly onto a severe varicose vein or you will cause pain and inflammation.

● Very gentle massage of the legs from the ankle to top of the thigh should be carried out daily, employing lots of effleurage. (1,2)
● Massage your own legs if no one is available. (3)

Lemon and geranium essential oils are invaluable.

To 10 mls (two teaspoons) of carrier oil add:
2 drops of lemon
1 drop of geranium

OTHER ADVICE
● Include lots of garlic (especially raw) to improve the circulation.
● Eat lots of fresh fruit, especially blackberries, blackcurrants, citrus fruits, cherries, pineapples, rose hips and strawberries, to reduce the fragility of the blood vessels.
● Vitamin C, E, ginkgo biloba and garlic capsules are all

excellent.
● Avoid standing for long periods of time.
● Elevate the legs higher than your head for about 15 minutes every day to improve drainage.

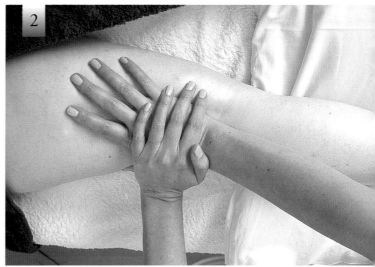

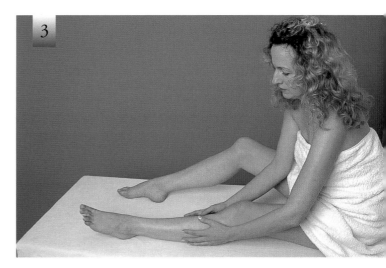

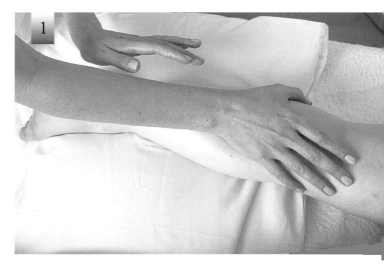

DIGESTIVE PROBLEMS

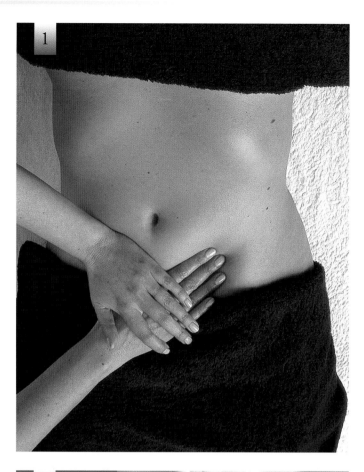

Many people suffer from digestive problems such as constipation, irritable bowel syndrome, indigestion and so on. Such disorders often originate from stress or from eating the wrong foods, inadequate intake of water, lack of exercise or even certain drugs.

MASSAGE TREATMENT

Massage of the abdomen is a highly effective treatment. If the problem is chronic then the abdomen should be treated daily until the bowel moments are regular. Then it should be carried out whenever necessary.

● Place one hand on top of the other on the navel and proceed to massage in a clockwise direction. Then put your three middle fingers at the bottom right hand side of the abdomen. Start to work slowly up the right hand side (ascending colon) with small gentle circular movements. (1)
● Continue working across the abdomen below the rib cage (transverse colon) and then turn and work down the left-hand side of the abdomen (descending colon). Slide lightly back to the lower right hand side and repeat several times. (2) Finish with some effleurage.

To enhance the massage use essential oils of peppermint and rosemary for constipation or chamomile and mandarin for conditions such as diarrhoea or irritable bowel syndrome to calm and soothe the colon.

OTHER ADVICE
● Eat a healthy high fibre diet to increase the frequency and quality of bowel movements.
● Drink 6-8 glasses of water per day.
● Avoid prolonged use of laxatives, which make the bowel lazy.
● Do not ignore the urge to move your bowels.
● Avoid stress.
● Drink peppermint, fennel or chamomile tea.

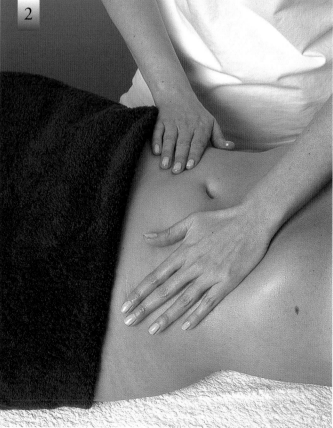

GENITO-URINARY PROBLEMS

FLUID RETENTION

Fluid retention is particularly common in the legs, especially around the ankles, although it may also be present around the wrists. Most elderly people will experience some fluid retention. Massage is a highly effective way of helping to drain away accumulated lymphatic fluid.

MASSAGE TREATMENT

● If the swelling is around the ankles, begin with gentle effleurage of the whole leg from ankle to thigh. Perform gentle circular friction movements around the ankle. (1)

● Then gently mobilise the ankle by rotating it clockwise and anti-clockwise. (2)

● For puffiness around the wrists, effleurage up the entire arm from wrist to shoulder. Then perform small pressure circles around the wrists and gently circle them clockwise and anti-clockwise. (3)

To help to reduce the fluid, essential oils of geranium, lemon, mandarin and rosemary are all effective.

To 10 mls (two teaspoons) of carrier oil add:
2 drops of geranium
1 drop of lemon

OR

to 10 mls (two teaspoons) of carrier oil add:
2 drops of mandarin
1 drop of rosemary

OTHER ADVICE

● Drink at least 6-8 glasses of water daily.
● Avoid standing for long periods of time.
● Rotate the ankles/wrists as often as possible.
● Elevate the legs higher than the head twice daily if possible for at least 15 minutes to assist drainage.
● Eat plenty of garlic.
● Reduce salt.

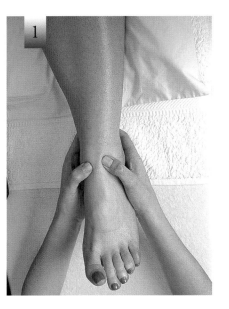

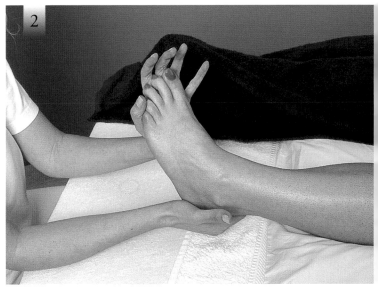

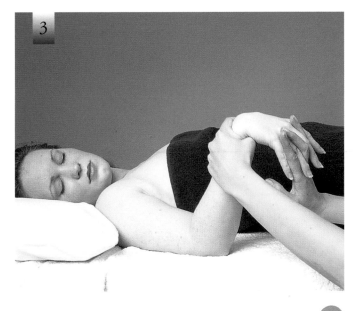

PRE-MENSTRUAL SYNDROME

Hundreds of symptoms have been attributed to PMS although the main ones include anxiety and mood swings, bloating of the abdomen and general fluid retention.

MASSAGE TREATMENT

Therapeutic massage can help to treat both the physical and emotional symptoms of PMS.

A full body massage should be carried out one or two days prior to the onset of the symptoms to help the woman to relax and balance the emotions. Many women feel as if they are retaining lots of fluid in the abdomen.

Gentle effleurage and stroking in a clockwise direction can be helpful.(1)

Pulling up the sides of the abdomen down towards the bladder can alleviate this problem. (2)

For maximum benefit add essential oils of chamomile, geranium, lavender or mandarin to the carrier oil. These oils are excellent for balancing the hormones as well as for minimising excessive fluid. In addition to therapeutic massage 6 drops of any of the above oils should be added to the bath daily.

OTHER ADVICE

● Reduce salt, sugar, caffeine and alcohol.
● Increase fibre intake.
● Try supplements of B complex and evening Primrose oil.
● Relax with yoga, Tai Chi or meditation.

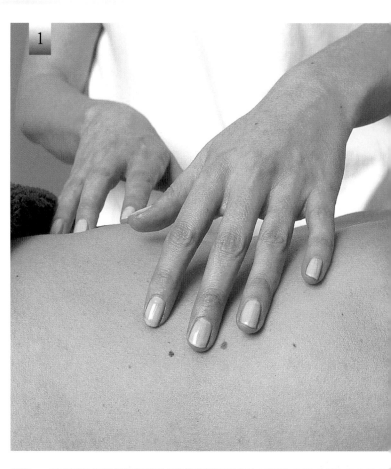

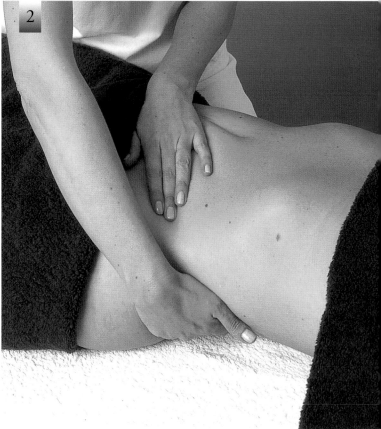

THE HEAD

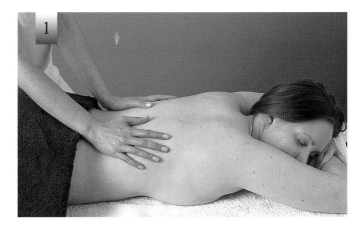

HEADACHES AND MIGRAINE

Headaches are caused by many factors ranging from muscular tension in the neck and shoulders, food allergies, eye strain, sinusitis, hormone imbalances and so forth. Therapeutic massage is very effective in the treatment of headaches since it is the best way of relieving stress and keeping the neck and shoulder muscles relaxed.

MASSAGE TREATMENT

Effleurage the whole back, paying particular attention to the upper back. Then perform small deep circular movements around the shoulder blades breaking down any knots and nodules that you may find. (1)

Knead the shoulders thoroughly squeezing and releasing with alternate hands and gently squeeze the neck muscles.

● Ask the receiver to turn over and effleurage both sides of the neck. (2)

● Then friction the base of the skull.(3) Stretch the neck carefully.

● Finally stroke outwards across the forehead to release any remaining tension. (4)

Essential oils of lavender and peppermint are a good combination. Use 2 drops of lavender and 1 drop of peppermint to 10 mls (2 teaspoons) of carrier oil. If the pain is severe then put 3 drops of lavender and 3 drops of peppermint into a small cereal bowl of lukewarm water and place a flannel in it to make a compress. Either place it on the forehead or on the back of the neck for maximum relief.

OTHER ADVICE

● Reduce stress
● Apply self massage to the neck and shoulders daily.
● Avoid foods, which may cause a headache – the main culprits are cheese, chocolate and red wine.
● B complex and zinc and are excellent for stress relief.

MUSCULO-SKELETAL PROBLEMS

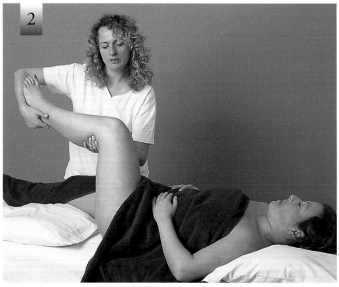

OSTEOARTHRITIS

This is a very common ailment caused by wear and tear, which affects primarily the weight bearing joints –the knees, and hips.

MASSAGE TREATMENT

Therapy is aimed at relieving stiffness, reducing pain and improving flexibility of the affected joints. It is a good idea to administer a full treatment every two weeks and to massage the arthritic joints daily. Remember that if a joint is very swollen you should never massage directly on to the inflamed area – work above and below the swelling.

● When treating arthritis of the knee, first effleurage the whole leg from ankle to the top of the thigh. Then effleurage the front of the thigh firmly.

● Gently friction around the knee cap to keep the patella freely movable. (1)

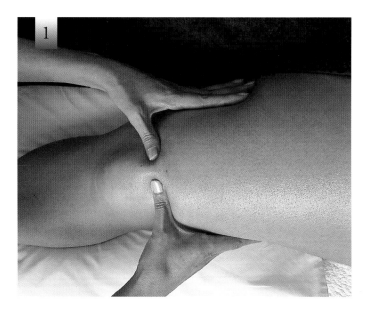

● Finally bend and stretch the knee slowly and carefully to maintain and increase the range of movement. (2,3)

Useful essential oils include chamomile (if there is inflammation), eucalyptus (pain relief), lavender (relaxing, pain relief), lemon (reduces a fluid and helps clear waste products), peppermint (pain relief, cooling) and rosemary (improves circulation, gets rid of toxins, pain relief). Add 3-4 drops of any of the above to 10 mls of carrier oil. If pain is severe then a compress can be made by sprinkling 6 drops of essential oil into a bowl of lukewarm water, soaking it up with a flannel and placing it on the affected area.

OTHER ADVICE

● Keep to your recommended weight.
● Try selenium ACE.
● Take gentle exercise such as yoga and Tai Chi or walking to keep the joints mobile.

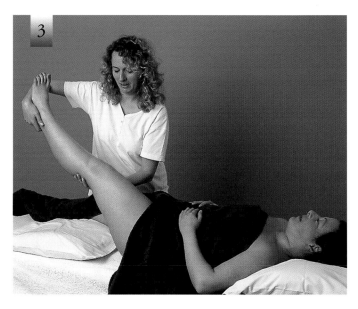

For details of how to massage other joints follow the step-by-step sequences described in previous chapters and use the self-massage routines daily.

RESPIRATORY PROBLEMS

ASTHMA/COUGHS/NASAL CONGESTION

Asthma is characterised by wheezing caused by inflammation of air passages in the lungs which narrows the airways and reduces airflow in and out of the lungs. Stress and allergies such as pollen, house dust, certain foods etc may induce an attack.

MASSAGE TREATMENT

● Therapeutic massage will be concentrated upon the chest and upper back. Place the hands in the centre of the chest and effleurage outwards to open up the chest and encourage deeper breathing. (1)

To further release the chest place the heels of your hands so that they are cupped over the shoulders. Press down and hold for five seconds and repeat several times to open out the chest. Encourage the receiver to take a few deep breaths to encourage full inhalation and exhalation. (2)

Congestion in the chest may be relieved with percussion movements. Cup and hack over the back of the rib cage to stimulate the respiratory system and to loosen mucus and phlegm from the bronchial tubes.

Essential oils of eucalyptus and rosemary are particularly effective for bronchial congestion. Lavender helps to promote sleep and boosts the immune system, encouraging healing to take place. Lemon can break down mucus and fights off infections in the respiratory tract. A good chest rub would be:

To 10 mls (two teaspoons) of carrier oil:
1 drop of eucalyptus
1 drop of rosemary
OR
2 drops of lavender
1 drop of lemon

If someone is having an asthma attack and is very tense and panicky then put a couple of drops of lavender onto their palms and encourage them to breathe deeply.

● For nasal congestion therapeutic massage is excellent. Pay particular attention to the forehead, cheeks and nose area. (3)

Add 2 drops of lavender and 1 drop of rosemary to 10 mls of

carrier oil for a de-congestive facial blend. Also sprinkle a few drops of eucalyptus or rosemary onto a handkerchief and place it in your pocket so that you can inhale the aroma all day long.

OTHER ADVICE

● Avoid stress which can precipitate an asthma attack and depletes the immune system, making you more susceptible to coughs and colds.

● Eliminate or at least cut down on dairy foods which encourage the production of mucus. Eat lots of fruit, vegetables and salad.

● Eat garlic, preferably raw daily as it is 'nature's antibiotic'. Ginger helps to break down phlegm.

● Take vitamin C to prevent coughs and colds.

● Practice gentle exercise such as yoga, which includes lots of breathing exercises.

● Open a window at night whilst you are sleeping to ensure a good supply of fresh air.

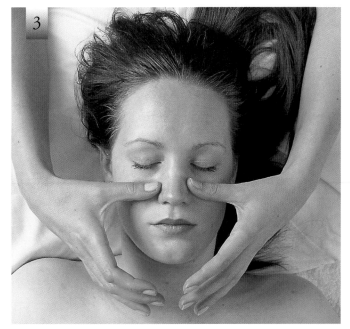

Conclusion

This book has hopefully made you aware of the enormous potential of the healing art of therapeutic massage. You will have found that giving a massage is as enjoyable and relaxing as receiving a treatment. To touch and to be touched is a fundamental and instinctive need in all of us regardless of age. The first sense that we develop is our sense of touch as the unborn child is constantly caressed inside the warmth of the mother's womb.

This close bond between mother and baby has a positive effect both physiologically as well as psychologically and children who grow up in families where there is deprivation of touch are generally more susceptible to physical and mental illnesses.

As we grow up, the majority of people seem to touch each other less and less. Most of us lose our intuitive sense of touch. This is a pity as therapeutic massage is an instinctive form of medicine. It has something to offer people of all ages. Hopefully this book has awakened and heightened your sense of touch. Massage your family and friends and spread the work about the magic of massage. Let therapeutic massage become part of your daily life and notice how relaxed, uplifted, balanced and rejuvenated you become.

If you intend to practice massage professionally then you must undertake training with a reputable establishment. A recognised professional training course will involve a thorough grounding in anatomy and physiology as well as practical tuition. Ensure that the course is accredited to a professional association, check out how long the school or college has been established and the qualifications and clinical experience of the principal tutor.

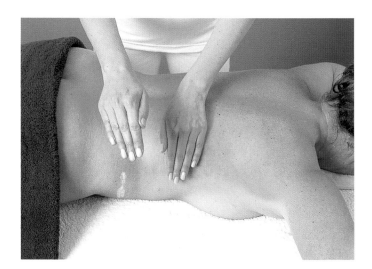

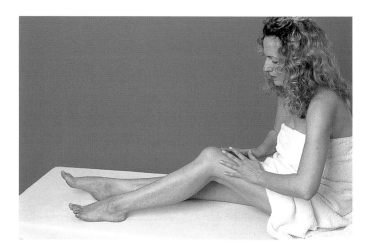

USEFUL ADDRESSES

United Kingdom

Beaumont College of Natural Medicine
Denise Whichello Brown
39 - 41 Hinton Road
Bournemouth
Dorset BH1 2EF
(44) 01202 708887
denisebrown@beaumontcollege.co.uk

International Therapy Examination Council
10/11 Heathfield Terrace
London W4 4JE
+44 (0) 20 8994 4141

USA

American Massage Therapy Association

Index

Picture credits
All pictures © Quantum Books Ltd.
Many thanks to models:
Maria, Mel and Sarah